WOOD BLOCKING AS REQUIRED

FACE OF FRAMING

FACE OF WOOD PANELING

* ENTASIS TO FRONT FACE OF PILASTER ONLY

⑤ PLAN DETAIL AT PILASTER FULL SIZE

TOP OF PILASTER DOTTED

5" AT CAP

6" AT BASE

6"

② ELEVATION AT BASE OF PILASTER FULL SIZE

LINE OF PLINTH

SQUARE PLINTH

* NOTE: SEE AT DWG #1

SQUARE PLINTH

CONTINUOUS CURVE TO COLUMN AND TO FRONT FACE PILASTER

③ PLAN DETAIL AT BASE OF COLUMN FULL SIZE

SQUARE PLINTH

TOP OF COLUMN DOTTED

* NOTE: 5" AT DINING ROOM

3" R. RADIUS AT BASE

2½" R. RADIUS AT CAP

④ REFLECTED VIEW AT COLUMN CAPITAL-EST.

TURNED

SQUARE

3"

① ELEVATION AT BASE OF COLUMN FULL SIZE

FAIRFAX & SAMMONS
ARCHITECTS P.C.
§

67 Gansevoort Street, New York, New York 10014 • TEL 212.255.0704 FAX 212.229.9517

Project: FARMLANDS, COOPERSTOWN
Sheet Title: LIBRARY PALLADIAN WINDOW DETAILS
Date: FEB. 7, 2000
Sheet No.: A-406.C
By: B.T.P.
Scale: FULL SIZE

AMERICAN HOUSES

THE ARCHITECTURE OF FAIRFAX & SAMMONS

AMERICAN HOUSES

THE ARCHITECTURE OF FAIRFAX & SAMMONS

MARY MIERS

Introduction by Adele Chatfield-Taylor

Principal Photography by Durston Saylor

CLASSICAL AMERICA

RIZZOLI
NEW YORK

First published in the United States of America in 2006 by
RIZZOLI INTERNATIONAL PUBLICATIONS, INC.
300 Park Avenue South, New York, NY 10010
www.rizzoliusa.com

ISBN-10: 0-8478-2857-3
ISBN-13: 978-08478-2857-9
LCCN: 2006928459

Text (except as noted below) © 2006 Mary Miers
Introduction © 2006 Adele Chatfield-Taylor

Front cover: A Federal-Style Country House (p. 8)
Back cover: An English Arts and Crafts-Style Country House (p. 72)
Page 1: A Georgian-Style Villa (p. 88)
Page 2-3: A British Colonial-Style Residence (p. 200)

Designed by Abigail Sturges

Printed and bound in China

2006 2007 2008 2009 2010/ 10 9 8 7 6 5 4 3 2 1

*This book is dedicated to the talented team of architects
in our office, the builders who make it a reality, and the
inspired patrons who share our vision.*

CONTENTS

INTRODUCTION

Adele Chatfield-Taylor

A country retreat in Virginia.

I first encountered the work of Richard Sammons and Anne Fairfax in New York City in the early 1990s. They had been hired to rescue and recast a nineteenth-century stable that had structural problems and ungainly twentieth-century renovations.

I followed the project as they—together with an unusually enlightened client—re-imagined the unpromising, quasi-commercial ground floor space, and opened it up to a tenderly conceived garden that was until then an unlovely concrete yard. They worked deftly to make it beautiful both inside and out. Furthermore, the end product looked as though it had always been there, which to me is the acid test.

It was clear that Fairfax & Sammons were for me. Since then, the years have passed, and they have worked on two much-loved domiciles for my husband and me—one a ramshackle apartment in Greenwich Village in New York, and the other a 1930s beach house on the Atlantic.

Along the way, I've watched with pleasure as their careers burgeoned and flourished. This book—*American Houses*—is a perfectly named testimony to what they have accomplished. Thanks to a wonderful text and dreamy photographs, it documents, through a sampling of their work, their deep feeling for American architecture, character, and style. On the one hand, they reveal Americans' love of comfort and informality; on the other, they capture our upright quality and conservatism.

It is rare that architects of their relative youth can have mas-

tered so much. But Fairfax & Sammons can change gears and styles with amazing agility. A casual perusal of these pages reveals that they have mastered the following styles: Jacobean, Arts and Crafts (English and American), Colonial Revival, Palladian, Greek Revival, Rustic Mediterranean, British Colonial, Anglo-Italianate, and Anglo-Caribbean, to name a few. But, in the words of Richard Sammons, "everything goes through Jefferson." Amen.

If this is their stylistic palette, their mastery of size and proportion is no less extravagant. They can build a tycoon's spread on a scale that rivals Hadrian's villa or a Middleburg hunting box that is a perfect hideaway.

The transformation of their own house embodies their ingenuity when they are combining the new and the old. They took on two neglected side-by-side Colonial Revival structures on a busy street in the heart of the Greenwich Village Historic District. When they started, each house had a nice front door and a friendly facade, but not much else; one was tiny and squirrelly, the other larger but dark. By the time they were through, this "odd couple" had been turned into an enchanting, multilevel, full-sized house with a kitchen big enough to cook and sit in and a drawing room that folded onto two terraces and a crescent shaped end. The whole is lavish enough to accommodate a large party or cozy enough to be a honeymoon cottage for two. It is just right for the extremes of New York City life.

A villa in Palm Beach.

The American houses of Fairfax & Sammons look as though they'll truly be lived in. One imagines the waxing and waning of families over time—through Thanksgivings, Christmases, and christenings—vibrant families that will grow with the generations. Pristine as the places may be now, one sees how they will accumulate pictures and books, woodpiles, umbrella stands, gardens, and the routines that establish the rights of way of a house, the ups and downs, ins and outs, worn spots and indelible paths.

The bedrooms are especially pretty with their bay windows and views, their ruffled curtains and bowed valances. One can almost taste the breakfast that is about to arrive on a tray—coffee steaming, soft-boiled egg upended in an old-fashioned egg cup reigning over it all, folded newspaper waiting, dogs trailing along behind. And there goes another heavenly, sun-filled Saturday morning. But what could be a better use of a beautiful house?

Although they both have Virginia roots, Richard grew up in Ohio and Anne in Hawaii. They met at the University of Virginia School of Architecture where each became imbued with old world classicism. Once they got together, they started a life of travel, study, and teaching. They have always relished learning local architectural history and savoring regional specialties.

Professionally, they are now hitting their stride, having carved out a niche for the firm that is not slavish to any one tradition but instead part of the pluralism that is the American stream. In fact, they are at their best when they depart slightly from the perfection of any ideal and design a building that is unique to its own client and moment.

Lillifields embodies this independence perfectly. At first glance it looks old, but up close it is beautifully alive and new. Tradition speaks in its lovely proportions, the cut of the bays, the shutters, and corners. But look again. It is wonderfully familiar, but original. It has never been done before. We want to go in.

Down the road, Litchfield, built around the same time, is another example of the same phenomenon. It is Classical and traditional but rugged and bold. It is new American design.

These are the creations of real twenty-first-century Americans, designed with real American architects. Turn the pages and feast your eyes.

The experience of life at its most delicious happens in beautiful houses, of any scale, any style, and any age, but they must be wonderfully designed to unlock and contain domestic bliss. Fairfax & Sammons know how to do that. They can imagine a new career for an old building without obliterating its personality or past, and when the task is a new building, they have a knack for realizing what the client has in mind. They can imagine it, design it, site it, and, if asked, handle the interiors and gardens! They have astute judgment about what is possible and good. Surely this is what one wants in an architect—not to mention a friend. Long may they wave!

A Federal-Style Country House

FARMLANDS

COOPERSTOWN, NEW YORK, 2002

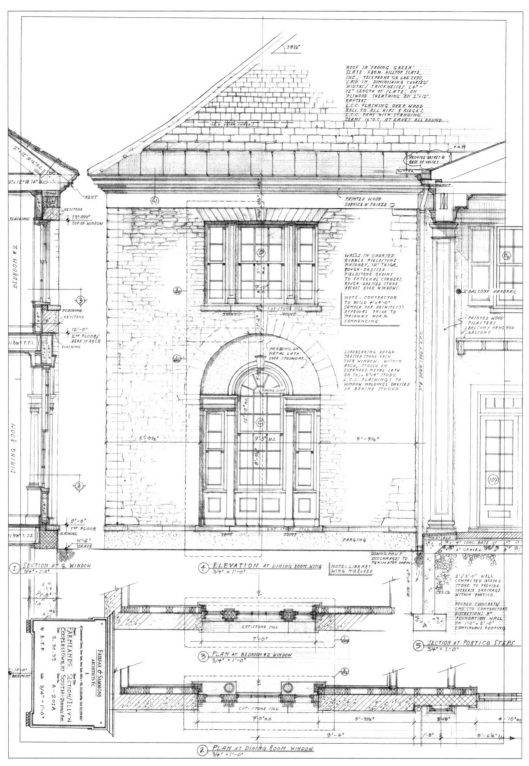

PREVIOUS PAGES *The south façade, overlooking Lake Otsego. The combination of local stone for the main block with shingled wings and slate roofs is typical of Federal period buildings in the area.*

ABOVE *Working drawing for entrance on north façade.*

FACING PAGE *Entrance, with door and doorcase salvaged from the earlier house that stood on this site.*

If one country house had to be chosen as an exemplar of Fairfax & Sammons's sophisticated interpretation of regional Classicism, it would surely be Farmlands in New York State. Surrounded by 600 acres of its own wooded estate, this Colonial Revival mansion looks so settled and well sited in its landscape, so rooted in the architectural tra-

ditions and materials of the locality, that it is difficult not to believe that it has been here since the early nineteenth century. Only closer inspection reveals that the high quality materials and beautiful craftsmanship are of recent vintage, and that the house is utterly in tune with modern standards of living.

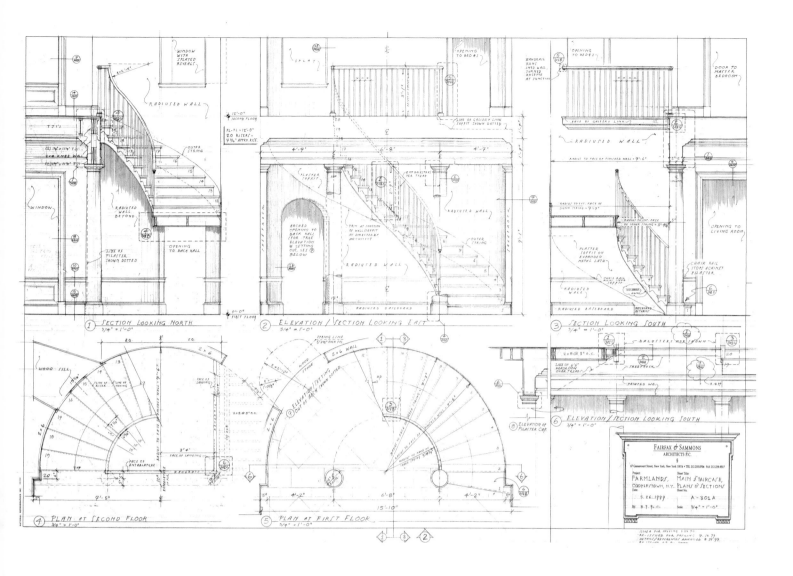

FACING PAGE *The limestone-paved entrance hall uses the Doric order for the chimneypiece and for the columns screening the circular staircase.*

ABOVE *Working drawing for staircase.*

RIGHT *Detail of wooden chimneypiece in the master bedroom; its Tower of the Winds order recalls that of the giant portico on the south elevation.*

13

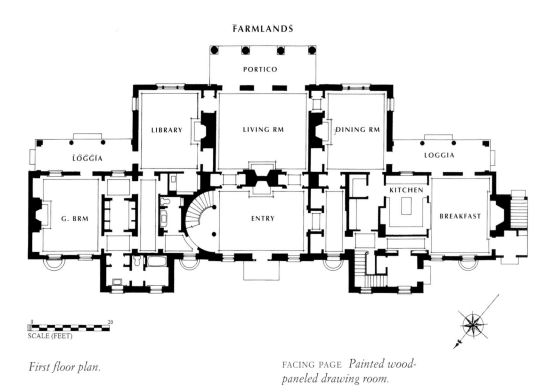

FARMLANDS

PORTICO

LIBRARY · LIVING RM · DINING RM

LOGGIA · LOGGIA

KITCHEN

G. BRM · ENTRY · BREAKFAST

0 20
SCALE (FEET)

First floor plan.

FACING PAGE *Painted wood-paneled drawing room.*

It was built to replace a nineteenth-century timber-framed summer residence that had been inherited by the owner, a scion of a great brewery, and, although larger, preserves something of the spirit of that earlier house, whose front door and doorcase it re-uses. The main walls are of lime-mortared coursed rubble stone, which gives the exterior its wonderful texture and variegated coloring of deep pinks and browns, the window arches and subtly graduated quoins being defined by larger blocks. The combination of this locally quarried bluestone with white painted timber for windows, columned porches and clapboarded wings, and New York slates for the roofs, is a feature of local buildings of the Federal period, such as Woodside Hall, which Richard Sammons has carefully observed. Many of these were put up by newcomers from Connecticut and New York, and they reflect the tradition of mixing unrendered coursed rubble masonry with timber Classical detailing—a practice that Farmlands revives. The use of local materials worked in a traditional manner gives the house its sense of durability and its feeling of belonging to the rugged landscape of the Mohawk Valley.

Cooperstown was the home of James Fenimore Cooper, and the surrounding area inspired several of his novels; indeed, Lake Otsego, which Farmlands overlooks, is the author's fictional Lake Glimmerglass in *The Pioneers* (1823) and *The Deerslayer* (1841). The house is carefully designed and orientated to take advantage of superb south facing views to this lake. It is entered on the more restrained north front—a carefully modulated Palladian composition with a pedimented cen-

terpiece—but the south front, also with a three-bay pedimented centerpiece, is the more imposing façade, conceived as a giant portico in the manner of Jefferson's pavilions at the University of Virginia, with columns bearing leaf capitals derived from the Temple of the Four Winds in Athens. An upper story porch provides the master bedroom with a private balcony overlooking the lake.

With its pair of flanking Palladian windows in round-arched recesses framing similar vistas for the dining room and library, this elevation is particularly resonant of the work of architects of the Federal period, such as Latrobe and Bulfinch. These rooms, with the drawing room at the center, form an enfilade of principal public rooms across the south front.

A dominant feature of the plan is the lateral spine wall containing the massive flue that heats the drawing room and entrance hall on their party wall. The hall to the north is a great double-height space that mirrors the drawing room on plan, in this respect echoing the equivalent room at Monticello, which Jefferson displayed as a natural history museum. But unlike Jefferson's Palladian practice of concealing the stairs, Farmlands makes a feature of them in the Federal manner. A flying staircase ascends to the galleried landing in an elegantly curved space, which opens off the east end of the hall through a columned screen.

The hierarchy of different spaces is reflected by the orders: Doric for the stone-floored hall, Ionic for the principal living rooms, and a simplified Greek Corinthian for the south-facing portico and master bedroom.

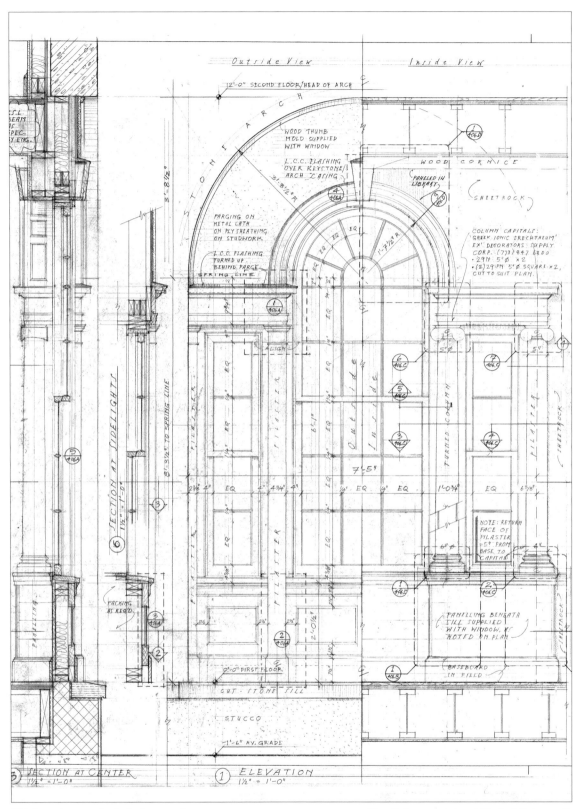

Working drawing for Palladian window.

FACING PAGE *The dining room's hand-blocked Zuber wallpaper has been lined up so that its imaginary landscape relates to the view seen through the Palladian window.*

FACING PAGE *The library, paneled with unpainted local white pine.*

ABOVE *Custom-made gun cabinet.*

The principal rooms are all contained in the compact main block. This reads almost as an independent entity when viewed from the south, for it stands well forward from the clapboarded wings, defined by the hipped form of its steeply pitched roof. The north front has a more formal feel, its horizontality emphasized by the unbroken succession of dark green shuttered sash windows ranging across all 13 bays.

The interior of Farmlands is distinguished by fine, crisply detailed millwork, the *piece de resistance* being the dining room's Serlian window, and its balancing pair in the library, which also has an Ionic chimneypiece. The library is fitted out with unpainted pine paneling, the drawing room with paneling painted a grey-green. In the dining room, the walls above the dado are hung with a French Zuber block printed wallpaper depicting a hunting scene. This has been carefully positioned so that the hills shown in the imaginary landscape continue the line of the hills seen through the window on the other side of the lake. Sally Dinkle Giordano of Leta Austin Foster was responsible for all the interior decoration.

19

*Breakfast/family dining room with exposed chamfered
ceiling beams of white oak. The kitchen is visible beyond.*

Breakfast/family dining room, with the buttery through the Dutch door on the right.

Private balcony to master bedroom overlooking Lake Otsego.

FACING PAGE *The south elevation, viewed from the lake.*

In the wings, which open onto south-facing loggias, there is a guest bedroom suite on the east side and the kitchen and breakfast room on the west, with bedrooms on the floor above. The kitchen and interconnecting paneled breakfast room introduce a less formal note, with a heavy beamed ceiling, a large, stone-cheeked open fireplace, and rustic furniture.

In their design for this house, Fairfax & Sammons have created a fitting centerpiece to a working sporting estate that restores faith in traditional architectural and rural values. With its hierarchy of spaces and functions, traditional architectural language, and strong relationship to the landscape, Farmlands is a rural retreat conceived in the manner of earlier country houses, whose owners identified with the land and the pleasures of outdoor pursuits. In this sense it belongs to a country house tradition that saw a renaissance at the beginning of the last century, when rich financiers bought land on which to build a mansion and engage in farming and rural sports. Farmlands demonstrates clearly how these values have a relevance today, and how a traditional-looking country house, for which the estate is still an essential element, can accommodate and enhance the contemporary lifestyles of its owners.

A CONNECTICUT VILLA

LILLIFIELDS
SOUTHPORT, CONNECTICUT, 1999

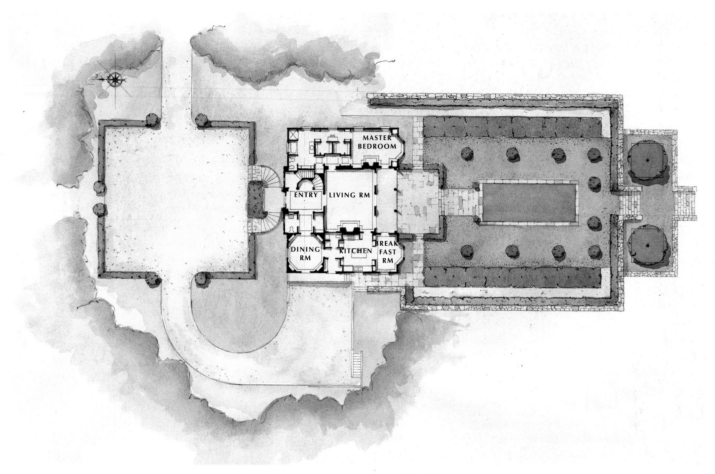

Among the many ports that punctuate the coastline of Connecticut, Southport is one of several small Colonial settlements that still has the appearance of a working harbor town, although it is now the preserve of well-heeled weekend leisure sailors. Founded on a flourishing maritime economy, it retains an impressive number of fine eighteenth- and nineteenth-century houses, many built for shipmasters, merchants, and captains by carpenter builders armed with pattern books, such as Asher Benjamin's *The American Builder's Companion* (1806). It is houses such as these, with their local building materials and subtle regional variations on the Greek Revival, Dutch, and other architectural styles, that have inspired a number of Fairfax & Sammons's projects. Notable among them is a modest-sized Palladian villa that stands on a small lot near Southport, among the former farmhouses and more recent neo-Classical residences that populate the wealthy wooded suburbs of Connecticut. Built for travel writer and interior decorator Nancy Marcantonio, Lillifields is smart and well proportioned, yet it possesses something of the reticence and anonymity of the Georgian vernacular that is so much a part of the character of a town like Southport.

Mrs. Marcantonio chose to collaborate with Fairfax & Sammons because she had heard of their conversance with the work of Thomas Jefferson and wished to emulate the pure Palladian spirit of Jefferson's little-known house, Edgemont in Virginia. Built in 1797 for James Cocke, Jefferson's only known timber-framed house has been described as "the epitome of everything that was most admired of Palladio in the New World, combining as it does simplicity with elegance, and beauty with convenience." By coincidence, Richard Sammons and Anne Fairfax had recently visited Edgemont when Mrs. Marcantonio first got in contact with them.

Like Edgemont, Lillifields is a simple understatement of a Palladian villa, with a compact six-room plan and a perfect geometric system relating to its every part. It, too, is wood-framed, with simple, clear-cut lines and understated ornament. Mrs Marcantonio wanted a relatively affordable house that would be small enough for just one or two people, yet comfortable enough to accommodate visiting family from time to time. She wanted it to function very much as a contemporary home, but to look as if it might always have been here.

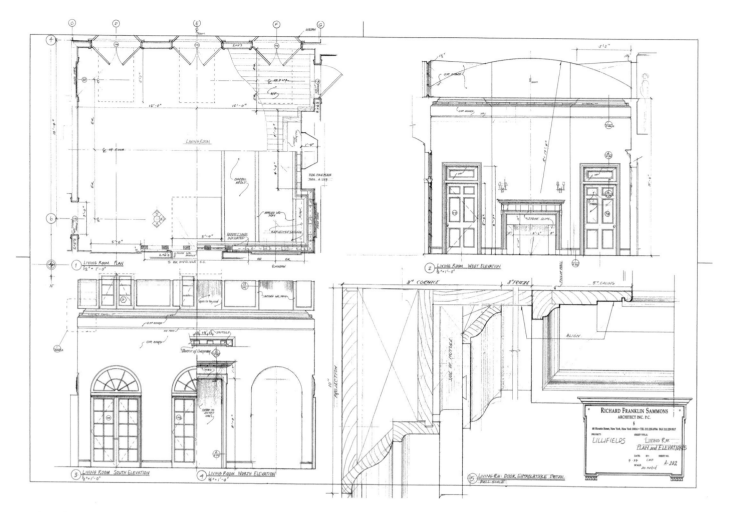

Working drawing for living room.

FACING PAGE *The double-height living room, with daylight flooding through windows cut into the barrel-vaulted ceiling. French doors open onto a loggia, with the garden beyond.*

The north entrance front is architecturally the more serious, introducing the Doric single story and attic scheme in a taut, sparely detailed tripartite façade that takes as its model the Villa Malcontenta near Venice. But there is also plenty of the local vernacular about Lillifields, with its characteristic juxta-position of flushboarded centerpiece (lined out to resemble ashlar, with wooden quoins imitating stone) and clapboarded outer bays. Beneath its shingled roof, the villa adopts the characteristic New England livery of white painted clapboard and bottle-green shutters. Special "restoration glass" has been used for the windows to add character and liveliness to the exterior.

The Federal-style influences first apparent on the entrance front—elegant sash windows and recurring elliptical forms (the leaded fanlight was made by a local blacksmith)—become stronger on the garden elevation. Here, a trio of round-arched openings leads onto a loggia-style porch. Playful ogee-roofed bay windows add a lighter touch, recalling the Regency Revival of the late 1920s–30s (their stylized keystone urns are among several Swedish Modernist influences that have crept in). One local architect who was designing unpretentious houses in a stripped-down Colonial style at that period was Royal Barry Wills (1895–1962), whom Richard Sammons much admires.

Wills's signature chimneys are echoed on the garden front at Lillifields, where a pair of similarly massive structures in white-washed brick rise through the roof slope.

Although the plot extends to only two acres, the house stands in the middle of a gentle incline surrounded by a grove of wild ash and cherry, so that it feels more rural than it actually is. The slope has allowed garaging to be excavated into the basement, and the garden to be terraced on several levels. To provide for a south-facing garden, Fairfax & Sammons turned the house so that the front door faces away from the street, and cut the garden into the hillside, shielding it from the road with extensive drystone garden walls. The landscape architect Charles Stick designed the garden in an Italianate manner to reflect the symmetry and order of the house. The long reflecting pool down the center is painted grey to give a blue-grey depth to the water, and outlined by spherical boxwood bushes.

The plan, with principal rooms and master bedroom suite arranged around three sides of a central living space, fulfils an important condition of the project—that corridors be mini-mized in the interests of good circulation, and that the master bedroom open directly onto the garden. Despite its depth, the house is very transparent, with a view right through to the gar-

Kitchen, with breakfast room beyond.

FACING PAGE *The octagonal dining room, which doubles as a library.*

den from the front door. The vestibule, painted a stone color and lined out to resemble ashlar, is a perfect neo-Classical stair hall. An elegant stair sweeps up in a semi-circular curve beyond a screen of Tuscan columns, which is balanced by pilasters on the other side. A small lobby, flanked by closet and powder room, leads through to the dining room on the right.

Ahead lies the living room, which was conceived as a daily living space at the heart of the house, rather than as a room to be used only for formal occasions. Rising full height beneath a shallow vault, this room, with its deeply projecting mutule cornice, is the only one to repeat the full Doric entablature of the exterior (elsewhere inside the baseless Tuscan order is used). Its connection with the outside is also emphasized by the light pouring through the attic casements and by the trio of French doors, which give it something of the feel of a garden room. The upper clerestory counteracts the effect of the loggia—a

Colonial-style feature with tin roof and brick paving that considerably reduces the penetration of sunlight into the lower half of the room. On the right of the fireplace, a dummy door has been inserted to maintain the symmetry, and there are subtle repetitions of properly detailed and proportioned architectural moldings, such as in the design of the chimneypiece.

The dining room is suitably Jeffersonian in spirit, being an octagonal room on the northwest corner, claret-colored above cream-painted dado paneling. Equipped with integral bookcases, it doubles as a library, and there are storage closets hidden behind jib doors on four walls. It leads through to the kitchen and breakfast room on the west side of the house, the former designed by Mrs. Marcantonio with modern equipment discreetly contained. Her continental tastes are reflected in the furnishings and interior decoration throughout the house, which were all her work.

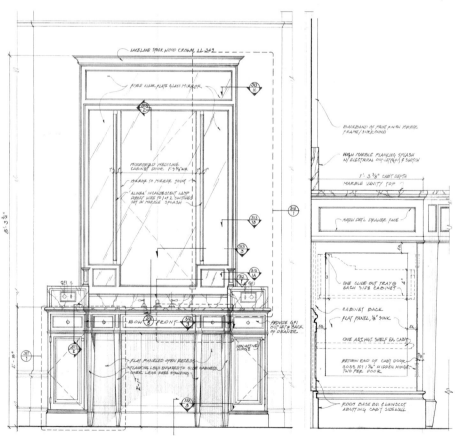

TOP *Master bedroom, with a bay window opening onto the garden and its own separate door to the loggia.*

BOTTOM *Working drawing for bathroom vanity cabinet.*

FACING PAGE *Master bathroom, with painted millwork and a floor of American white oak.*

ABOVE *Working drawing for the rear loggia.*

RIGHT *View of the south façade from the garden.*

The master bathroom, on the left of the vestibule, is
screened from outside view by mirrored shutters. Its diminutive vault echoes the living room ceiling, and the sunken, mar-
ble-topped bath within a mirrored alcove is supported on a
low socole, or Greek-style pedestal. Between this room and the
master bedroom is an anteroom with recessed cupboards,
which serves as a dressing room. The attic story, lit by casement windows, accommodates the guest bedrooms and bathrooms. From the landing it is possible to look down onto the
vaulted living room through openings that cut into the
vaults—a direct reference to the Palazzo Massimo in Rome.

There is nothing ostentatious about Lillifields; it is a sensi-
tive work for a likeminded client, built with materials and
skills of the highest quality to suggest something of the distinctive local yet anonymous character of New England's traditional provincial craftsmen. The architecture springs from a scholarly understanding of the work of Jefferson, overlaid by influences from architects such as the Virginian Milton Grigg, who
in the 1920s and 30s revived the spirit of the great master by
building modern villas in his style, and by carrying out sympathetic restorations of his work.

34

AN OLD ENGLISH REVIVAL
COUNTRY HOUSE

ETHANDUNE
BEDFORD, NEW YORK, 1995

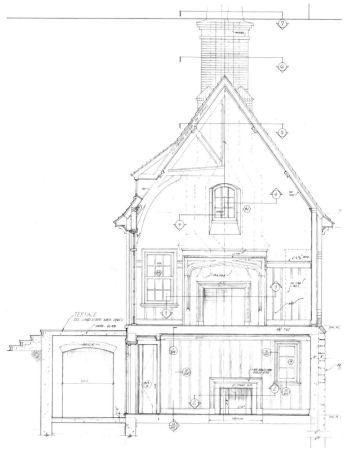

Reminiscent of a half-timbered Old English manor house, Ethandune lies hidden down a rough track in its own 48 acres of wooded park north of Bedford. This area was farmed until the 1930s, but has since become thickly wooded again, as it was in the seventeenth century. It is good riding country, with horse trails winding through the trees between intermittent rocky outcrops—an ideal location for a country retreat that does not feel encroached upon by suburbia, yet is not too far from the city.

Ethandune's mellow, weathered-looking exterior belies its 1929 date. The architect Kerr Rainsford designed it as his own home on land given as a wedding present by his in-laws, who lived in a neighboring house. His wife was the poet Christina Rainsford, a correspondent of, among others, the English writer and member of the Bloomsbury Group, Vita Sackville West. After Rainsford's early death, Christina lived on here as a widow until she died at the age of 100 in 1995, after which the house was sold to the present owners, whose backgrounds are in media and law.

Recognizing the historic interest of this largely unaltered house, but wishing to renovate and modernize the existing accommodation, and to build on a large family room and make other additions, the owners commissioned Fairfax & Sammons to come up with a sympathetic scheme. The architects assured the Rainsfords' daughter, Rita Rouner, who has shared with the present owners many secret pleasures of the estate, that they would preserve the integrity of her father's house, and they have kept to this promise. They have designed a new wing that complements the Jacobethan/Old English Revival style and cottagelike scale that are so much part of Ethandune's charm.

The existing L-plan front is little altered. Rainsford, who graduated from the Ecole des Beaux Arts in 1911, worked on a number of local buildings, including the Katonah Library, and designed the Greek Orthodox cathedral in Manhattan. A highly romantic architect who favored an eclectic Old English style, he conceived Ethandune as a deliberate counterpoint to the formal appearance of his in-laws' adjacent, Georgian-style brick house, and indulged his taste for the whimsical. He added a half octagonal entrance/staircase tower with a dovecote in its upper stage (the dovecote has now been converted into a lantern to light the top of the stair), and mixed local materials to give the house a rustic Arts and Crafts feel. Walls of craggy field boulders give way to brick and half timbering on the upper floor; the roofs are made of clay pantiles (unusual for the United States), and some of the gables are weatherboarded.

Fairfax & Sammons's new wing runs back behind the gabled range on the right of the entrance front, reminding us of the significance of home and hearth in its emphasis on roof and fireplace. It is built of red brick, which, in keeping with

FACING PAGE *New kitchen, with windows wrapping round three sides of an octagon, glazed roof, and a lantern, which also functions as a vent.*

ABOVE *View of kitchen addition from exterior, located in the angle of the existing building and the new wing.*

the Jacobethan style, is particularly beautifully detailed on the gable end with brick diapering and inset stone roundels. The red tiled roof is enlivened with Tudor-style chimneys and a pretty Gothic ventilation fleche. Inside, the family room is conceived as a great hall, with an open king post truss roof made of heavy, hand-hewn pine timbers. This is pegged in the traditional manner, and carefully pitched to observe the correct Gothic proportions. Windsor chairs, old tables, chests, rugs, and other antiques are mixed with comfortable contemporary furnishings.

The need to admit as much daylight as possible into this new wing (which projects to the northeast) was addressed by angling it at 45 degrees to the existing range, and by inserting windows of varying scales at different levels. Thus, diminutive catslide dormers let daylight in through the roof; the east wall has a tall, canted bay window; French doors run along the

west wall, and there are two windows in the gable end—one in the thickness of the chimneybreast. And finally, there is even a small window to light the inside of the inglenook fireplace. A handsome, Tudor-arched chimneypiece of pale limestone dominates the far wall, the Gothic detailing of its cornice crown copied from Rainsford's chimneypiece in the drawing room. Paneled walls and other timber work in this room are painted cream, a palette chosen by the English interior decorator Keith Irvine of Irvine and Fleming, who was responsible for the Fairfax & Sammons schemes and new furnishings throughout the house.

Because of the sloping site, the new wing is raised up on a battered basement plinth of rugged stone, buttressed on the north elevation by the massive, stepped brick chimneybreast of the family room fireplace. This raised basement has provided space for a children's den and exercise room. The landscape

ABOVE *New garage and staff quarters in a detached cottage with a jerkin-head roof and waney wood weatherboarding.*

RIGHT *View of house from pool.*

architect Ben Page of Nashville, who conceived the masterplan for the estate, was responsible for the huge, west-facing terrace off the family room, as well as the siting of the swimming pool and various ancillary buildings in the grounds.

In the angle at the intersection of the original building and the new wing, a spacious new kitchen has been created. This takes the form of a glass and timber half octagon with a glazed roof and lantern, so that it resembles a conservatory flooded with natural daylight. It is typical of Fairfax & Sammons's kitchens in combining their full repertory of cupboards and drawers—well-made and detailed in the traditional manner—with an array of state-of-the-art domestic equipment. The kitchen opens up the internal space, marking the transition from original house to new wing. The relationship between the two resolves itself on a single column.

Fairfax & Sammons have made some modest interventions to the existing house. These include a new powder room and a marble-lined master bathroom. There is also a flower room and new boot room, with ceilings molded into the forms of a St. George's cross and a St. Andrew's cross, respectively. The architects also turned their hands to ancillary buildings, designing a charming greenhouse and a detached garage and staff quarters disguised as an artistic cottage. This has a jerkin-hooded tiled roof and rustic stone walls between roughly sawn flanks weatherboarded in waney wood. It is a charming building, which shows a subtle appreciation of the picturesque qualities of the English Arts and Crafts vernacular, and demonstrates how equally confident the architects can be designing practical buildings in a vernacular idiom, as they are when creating more substantial buildings in a Classical manner.

A Shingle-Style
Country House

Greenwich, Connecticut, 1995

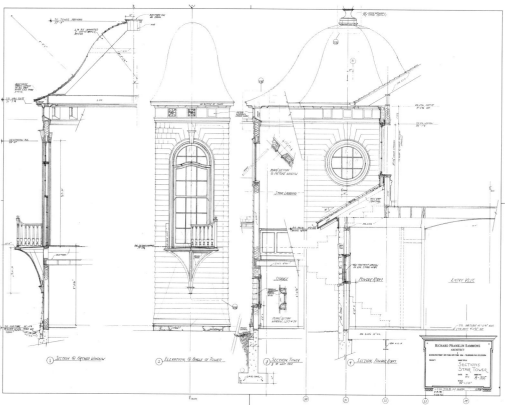

PREVIOUS PAGES *Entrance elevation.*

TOP *Site plan.*

ABOVE *Working drawing for stair tower.*

FACING PAGE *Stair tower with pulpit balcony,
vousoir shingles around the window heads, and a
metope clerestory lighting the stairwell.*

The story of this house on the Conyers Farm estate in
up-country Greenwich is that of an inspired rescue bid
to salvage an ill-conceived building. The resulting
Shingle-style country retreat is a brilliant transformation by
Fairfax & Sammons of a half-finished house of circa 1988.
Their first large commission was completed under budget and
to an impressively fast-track schedule.

Conyers Farm was subdivided in the 1980s, when parcels of
land were sold off separately and developed with a series of
large houses surrounded by their own 20 acres or more of
wooded parkland and paddocks. This is gated community
living on a grand scale, each property benefiting from the
shared privacy and jointly managed amenities of a beautifully
maintained landscape protected by security gates. The over-

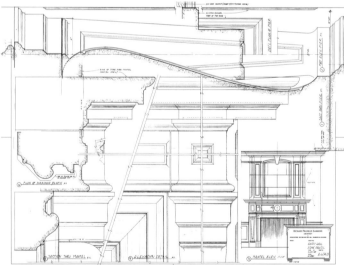

TOP *Entrance or living hall looking toward staircase.*

ABOVE *Working drawing of hall chimneypiece.*

RIGHT *Limestone chimneypiece in double-height entrance hall, with paneling of limed white oak.*

FACING PAGE *Living room with heavy wooden-beamed ceiling, looking out to the garden through a segmental arch.*

ABOVE *Winter family room.*

all feeling is that of a large, privately owned estate.

The former owners of the property had commissioned a Californian architect to build a Prairie-style house described by Richard Sammons as suggestive of "Frank Lloyd Wright on steroids." Dark and heavily overhung, this vaguely Oriental-looking building appeared awkward and unwelcoming; it was also badly planned and paid no regard to the East Coast climate. Not surprisingly, perhaps, it had been abandoned when the present owners acquired the site.

They commissioned Fairfax & Sammons to remodel the house, working to a strict budget. So Richard Sammons decided that, rather than fighting against it, he would work with the existing design, looking to some of Lloyd Wright's antecedents, such as Henry Hobson Richardson (one of America's first Beaux Arts trained architects), whose general approach provided inspiration. The house that emerged incor-

porated the bones of the earlier structure on a similar footprint, but with a new interior, and the exterior transformed into an eclectic Shingle-style composition with confidently handled Classical detail. The house has a deeply overhanging eaves cornice with stretched mutules in the manner of St. Paul's in Covent Garden, London, and a Doric columned portico inspired by Ernest Newton, an architect Richard Sammons much admires. Shallow pitched, oversailing roofs, and eyebrow dormers are features favored by Richardson, and there are references too, in the tall chimneys, to the English Arts and Crafts domestic style.

The entrance is on the west side, where originally there was a brutal stone excresance. The grandly scaled replacement portico has a shallow vault, its frieze and dramatically oversailing mutule cornice rising gently with the curve of the roof. This profile—a shallow, segmental arch—is used as a recurring

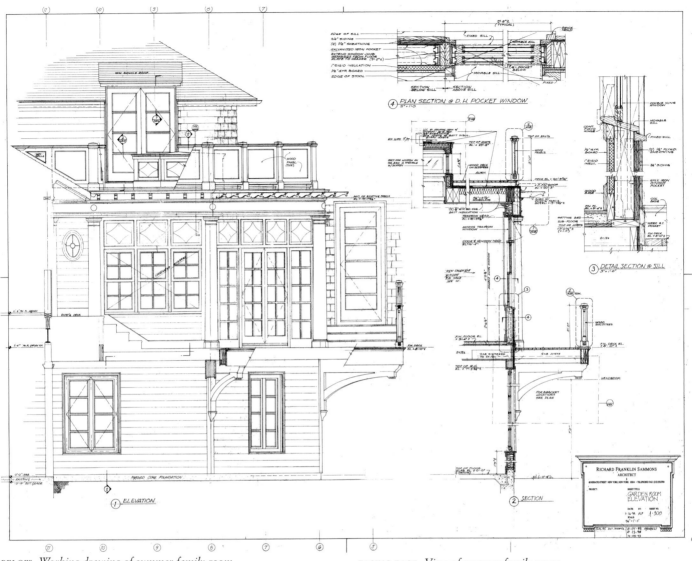

BELOW *Working drawing of summer family room.*

FACING PAGE *View of summer family room.*

motif throughout the house: in the architrave of the window above, for instance, and the lift of the eyebrow windows in the roof; in the overmantle of the great hall fireplace and the curve of the vaulted dining room.

The long, low, horizontal emphasis of the composition lacked a counterpoint, so in the remodeling a half-octagonal stair tower with an ogee roof was introduced on the entrance front to provide a gentle vertical emphasis. Tucked into the angle between the portico and the main block, this has helped to resolve some of the constraints of the existing design. Classical detail includes the large, round-arched window on the outer face of the tower (with the added whimsical touch of a pulpitlike balcony), flanked by occuli. A metope clerestory allows light to stream down into the stairwell, the tiny windows being tilted slightly so that they can be seen inside from the bottom of the stairs, as well as reflecting light more effectively into the enclosed stair hall.

Combining areas of granite masonry with some clapboard-

ing, the house is faced with coursed shingles, which are cut as voussoirs round the tower windows. The timber has been stained dark so that the substantial bulk of the building appears slimmer, the windows and other architectural details being picked out in white. A wall across the forecourt also helps to reduce the feeling of bulk, for, with its asymmetrical plan and skirt of separately roofed ground floor rooms projecting out from the main wall like glazed-in porches, the house is really quite large and rambling.

The interior has been gutted and redesigned with Classical proportions and detail to enhance the grand internal scale. The entrance leads into a double-height living hall on the east/west axis—a great central space with a galleried landing, beamed ceiling and wainscoting of limed white oak. Light floods down from the integral stair tower onto a floor of limestone flags inset with black marble tiles. The tour de force is the chimney-piece, with benches built into paneled sitting areas on either side, an original design by Richard Sammons. Its Doric archi-

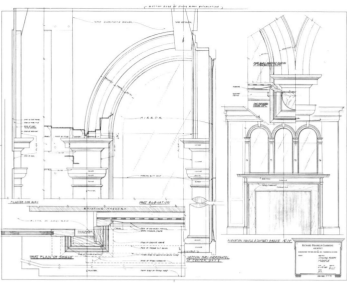

ABOVE *Working drawing of dining room chimneypiece, showing triple-arched overmantle inspired by Ernest Newton.*

RIGHT *Dining room with shallow, segmental vault and high painted wainscot paneling.*

trave echoes that of the porch, and the overmantle has a raised, segmental arched panel, which repeats the form of the door opening on the gallery landing above. In the paneling above the lefthand seating area, a small window peeps through into the passageway behind.

The architects and their clients have created an interior that blends smartness and informality. South of the hall, running west from the garden front, are the winter family room—with a central hearth and tray ceiling—the games room (with bar), the media or cinema room, and the guest quarters. To the north, aligned on the great central fireplace, runs the main corridor—a transverse passage with a series of shallow vaults, which opens directly into the living room and dining room and leads to the kitchen quarters, garage, and summer family room. The principal public rooms face the garden and have fireplaces on their party wall and generous fenestration. The floors are of pegged American white oak—a good renewable resource, with a density that responds well to staining. The timbers are quarter-sawn to random widths, which results in a wonderful texture.

The living room, with a coffered, wooden-beamed ceiling and a marble chimneypiece carved in Italy to Fairfax & Sammons's design, opens out into the transverse corridor through openings that repeat the segmental arch motif. The dining room has columned screens at each end and employs a shallow segmental vault and mirrors in the Soanian manner. The overall feeling of this room, with its robust, triple-arched overmantle and paneling with a strigilated frieze, is that of the Classical Arts and Crafts style of Ernest Newton. The ceiling's cornice has a pulvinated frieze, reinforcing the theme of curved surfaces. Behind the paneling is a secret spiral stair leading down to a wine cellar—one of several clever devices

FACING PAGE *Garden façade viewed from pergola gazebo.*   ABOVE *Wisteria arbor pergola linking poolhouse pavilions.*

which the architects have incorporated discreetly into the design (others include Harman hinge doors which fit back into the wallspaces between rooms, a walk-in cold room, a dumb waiter, and a present-wrapping closet).

The owner's wife has worked closely with the interior designer Pat Healing on the decoration and furnishing of these rooms, which are traditional in spirit and include pieces of antique furniture. A notable feature, however, is the bold juxtaposition of works of art emanating from a very different tradition. Currently president of the Guggenheim board of directors, she has a large collection of Modern and contemporary paintings, drawings, sculptures, and contemporary photography, and she has risen bravely to the challenge of incorporating this striking artwork into Fairfax & Sammons's handsome Classical interiors.

A feature of this house, which emphasizes its Colonial Revival influences, is the imaginatively designed white painted timberwork on the exterior. The summer family room, which projects out over the caretaker's quarters as a wooden half octagon with a balustraded verandah supported on great curving brackets, was modeled by Anne Fairfax on a sun porch

seen on the Condé Nast house, a Colonial Revival building in New Jersey. The cornice bristles with a decorative band of outriggers, so that the whole structure suggests a glazed-in pergola, in an echo of two charming Tuscan columned pergolas in the garden. One of these links a pair of pyramid-roofed pool house pavilions. The other oversails a curved screen at the far end of the garden. This was conceived as a gazebo—a quiet place to sit and contemplate, with timber seats incorporated into latticework panels between granite piers.

All this has been designed by Fairfax & Sammons. The owner, a businessman who was federal budget director for former President Reagan, and is currently a partner in two private equity firms, took a great deal of interest in the garden design, working closely with the landscape architect Henry White of HM White Site Architects, and, for the flowers, with Lynn Reed of Timeless Gardens. The landscape has now had a decade to mature, softening the setting. As more plants have grown up the walls and the shingles have weathered to a dark silvery grey, the exterior of the house has taken on a timeless quality that belies the recent date of its construction.

57

LEFT *Rear view of pergola gazebo at east end of garden.*

TOP AND ABOVE *Pergola views.*

A GEORGIAN-STYLE ARTS AND CRAFTS HOUSE

THREE OAKS
GREENWICH, CONNECTICUT, 1997

PREVIOUS PAGES *Entrance façade.*

ABOVE *The new addition fits seamlessly into the existing house.*

airfax & Sammons's subtle extension to this handsome house in the Georgian Revival manner of the late English Arts and Crafts period blends seamlessly with Phelps Barnum's original design of circa 1930. The house was built for Robert Peckham Noble, one of two brothers who made their fortune developing the Lifesaver mint candy business. Noble moved to Greenwich in 1920 and a few years later acquired some farmland to the north. Here he built himself a new country house, eventually extending the property to 43 acres. He became a leading light in the local community, and he and his wife, Meta, were enthusiastic participants of the local hunt. Meta Noble was a keen gardener, and it was she who was responsible for the fine English-style garden at Three Oaks. The grounds were landscaped as a parkland setting for the house, with sweeping lawns and mature specimen trees.

The house, which replaced an old farmhouse, was named after three magnificent oaks that still stand on the site. Approached from the west through a forecourt defined by a low brick wall, it presents a widely spaced three-bay central block flanked by projecting wings, fenestrated with traditionally-made six-over-six or eight-over-eight sash windows with external louvered shutters. The upper floor windows are

tucked right up to the eaves cornice, emphasizing the depth of the overhanging hipped slate roof. It is a composition redolent of works by the English Arts and Crafts architect Ernest Newton, with its suggestion, but conscious avoidance of, strict symmetry, and its polite yet informal air. Barnum built the house of clinker brick, which gives the walls their rustic texture and natural mottled look. He enhanced this effect by applying a layer of whitewash to the brickwork, and then sponging it off. The resulting variegated color tones and weathered-looking patina belie the house's relatively recent date. Fairfax & Sammons went to great pains to source the right clinker brick for their extension, eventually finding a suitable match in a landfill in Colorado. With their concern for authentic materials, they took care also to use roof slates that would blend well with the originals—thick slabs as deliciously rugged as oyster shells—eventually finding a suitable match in a quarry in Vermont.

After Noble's death in the 1970s, the grounds were subdivided and the house sold off with about 10 acres of land. In 1996, the owners since that time commissioned Fairfax & Sammons to carry out a sympathetic extension to accommodate a larger kitchen/breakfast room, a family room, a billiards

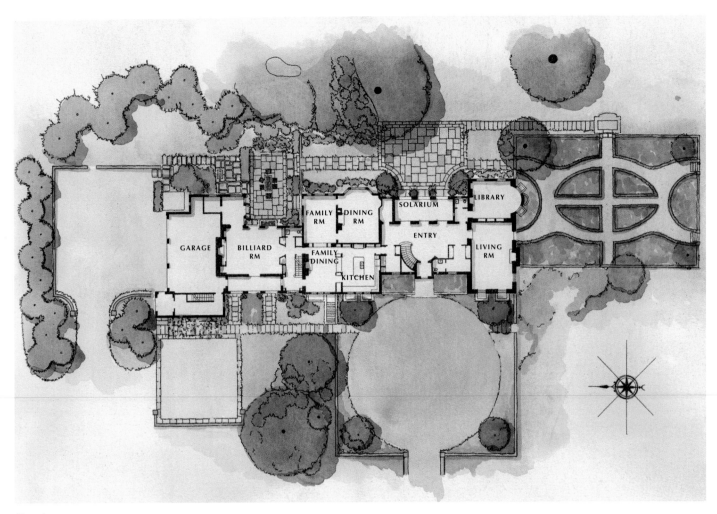

Site plan.

room wing with bedrooms above for their four sons, and a garage and staff accommodation. The architects' achievement is to have virtually doubled the size of the building without it being immediately apparent. Clever planning helps to integrate the two, resulting in a house that works well as a modern family home.

The original H-plan comprises a central block dominated by a transverse gallery/stair hall, with projecting wings containing the drawing room and bow-windowed library (on the right) and kitchen and dining room (on the left). The stair hall is approached through a vestibule, flanked on the right by a powder room and sitting room, and on the left by closets discreetly hidden behind the graceful curving sweep of the principal stair. Along the garden front is a loggia that had already been closed in; Fairfax & Sammons put new French doors into the round-arched openings and laid a stone floor to link it with the garden.

One of the features of this house is the excellent quality of its mahogany doors and other joinery, which includes antique architectural salvage introduced by Mrs. Noble with the help of Chicago architectural advisors Watson and Bowler. The drawing room is fitted out with late-eighteenth-century Adam-style woodwork, including a chimneypiece, door frames and wainscoting from Han's Court, Upton-upon-Severn, in Worcestershire, England. The dining room is in a Colonial Revival style, with paneling (made for the room) lacquered green to the specifications of the interior decorator, Elizabeth Stewart, and an imported marble chimneypiece providing the perfect backdrop for antique furnishings. In the powder room, the walls are lined with genuine French *boiserie*.

Fairfax & Sammons's additions have been cleverly stitched onto the north side of the house: the gabled roof over the original kitchen wing now sweeps down in a catslide over the new breakfast room extension. This room has a stone and tile-cheeked fireplace, raised up so that it can be seen over the table. The floors are of old reclaimed pine timbers from the renowned timber installer Baba, and the kitchen fittings—paneled cupboards, drawers, and other ingeniously-planned storage units—are beautifully made and designed in a traditional style that works well with the latest domestic equipment in the way that Fairfax & Sammons does so well. The refrigerator surround simulates a chimneybreast, and planters have been built in to disguise the fact that the existing kitchen windows drop down below the level of the work surfaces, which are

LEFT *New billiards room with flower room/conservatory beyond. The fireplace recess has a drop-down screen for the projection of films.*

ABOVE *Painted brick loggia.*

made of the architects' favored Kirkstone from England. The attention to detail in Fairfax & Sammons's domestic joinery is unerring. It is evident, to no less a degree, in the back stair vestibule/mud room, where carefully profiled moldings define beadboarded paneling, bench, and stair arch. The stairs lead down to a wine cellar and exercise room, and up to the new bedroom wing, which has a small sitting room under the cat-slide roof. Here, in order to open up the space a bit and admit more light, turned columns replace solid wall round the corner of the room.

Below the new bedrooms is a large billiards room, again with reclaimed, hand-scraped floor timbers, and with a wide spanning, heavily coffered pine ceiling. This is ornamented with rope moldings and other details, and has tongue-and-groove boards salvaged from French box cars. The bolection

Drawing room. The late-eighteenth-century chimneypiece came from a house in England.

RIGHT *Dining room, with paneling made for the room in the 1930s.*

limestone chimneypiece is fitted into a shallow-arched recess, which has a screen that can be dropped down in front of the fireplace for the projection of movies. This end of the room, which opens onto a flower room/conservatory, is comfortably furnished, as is the rest of the house, by the decorator Elizabeth Stewart. On the garden front to the south, accessed from the dining room and breakfast room, is a new family sitting room, and at the far end of the billiards room is a three-car garage combined with staff apartment. The architects have risen to the challenge of the request for a "romantic garage": they have incorporated a birdhouse (designed by Seth Weine) over a keystone formed of slates laid on their sides at the apex of the gable, and introduced large scrolled brackets.

In the existing house, a degree of gentle updating has been carried out. The master bathroom has been designed with a double-basined cabinet of Russian style, along with a special, diminutive make-up area. Bathroom and dressing rooms have been fitted out with a plethora of specially designed vanity units, closets with mirrored double doors folding back into door jambs, chests of drawers and other units, all as intricately devised as ship's carpentry. An office has been made in the southwest room, the bookshelves along one wall broken up with two-panel doors to modulate the wall plane. A small lobby on the ground floor between the dining room and porch had provided the original house (which was built during Prohibition) with a discreet bar, disguised as a butler's pantry/flower room. This has now been refitted as an actual bar, with a Dutch door and decorative antique tiles reclaimed from the original house.

LEFT *Breakfast room with raised fireplace in a brick and slate surround.*

TOP *Kitchen.*

ABOVE *Mudroom.*

TOP *Working drawing for poolhouse.*

ABOVE *Fire and water: the poolhouse pavilions, flanking a central fireplace.*

FACING PAGE *View of poolhouse pavilion and rose garden from the master bedroom.*

Fairfax & Sammons designed the new swimming pool on a better site further from the house, replacing an earlier one. In the siting and landscaping of this new pool and its attendant buildings, they worked closely with the English landscape architect, Peter Cummin of Cummin Associates. The changing room and kitchen are playfully conceived as a pair of classically detailed pagoda-roofed pavilions, built all of brick and slates to match the house, and linked by a pergola and a screen wall with reversed arches. These flank a central hearth, playfully suggesting the connection between the elements of fire and water.

Mr. Cummin was responsible for all the landscaping around the house. He redesigned the entrance court and garage area, and made the new terraces along the garden front, and the perennial garden around the new pool. The original English-style garden to the south of the house, designed by society landscape designer, Marian Coffin, has been reinstated, and the boxwood garden below the kitchen tidied up from a neglected state. Surviving from when the garden was created in the 1930s is the walled garden, with boxwood hedges in-filled with perennials, and a sunken fountain garden and orchard. The hallmarks of Peter Cummin's work are eminently suited to Fairfax & Sammons's philosophy, and they have worked together on other projects (see Litchfield, page 88). Cummin's gardens are conceived with absolute respect for the existing architecture, and designed to look as if they have always been there.

An English Arts and Crafts-Style Country House

LAKE WACCABUC
SOUTH SALEM, NEW YORK, 2000

At the core of this superbly sited country house in North Westchester County is a building of 1919 by Harrie T. Lindeburg. It was designed in a style reminiscent of the work of C. F. A. Voysey (1857-1941), the English Arts and Crafts architect whose simple but distinctive domestic architecture, furniture, and textile designs remained faithful to the Gothic ideal. Richard Sammons is a great admirer of Voysey, who was quoted as saying, "To be true to your material, true to your conditions, true to your highest instincts, is the surest and only way to true art."

The house had been poorly renovated over the years, and by the 1990s was distinctly down at the heels. Its present owners, a leading financial expert and his wife, chose Fairfax & Sammons from three competing firms to remodel and substantially enlarge the building in a style that maintained its original Arts and Crafts character.

The house is built on a bluff, from where it enjoys fine, uninterrupted views eastwards over Lake Waccabuc to the rolling wooded country beyond. To accommodate new principal rooms, Fairfax & Sammons added a large, cruciform wing to the south, positioning it at a slight angle to the existing building so that it would benefit from the views over the lake. On the west entrance front they rebuilt the porch to a design inspired by another English Arts and Crafts architect, W. R. Lethaby. This is robustly detailed, with Gothic profiles to the rafter ends and contrasting bandings of exposed bluestone at the imposts and base.

Site plan.

Entry vestibule with Dutch door.

The juxtaposition of materials and external finishes on this house is subtly handled, both to work well color-wise and to impart a suitably rustic air. The external timber paintwork echoes the blue-green of the slates, and the walls are rough rendered and whitewashed, with areas of coursed local granite rubble left exposed. This is particularly effective at the south end, where the house is built out on a craggy rampart of exposed masonry over steeply dropping ground. Cleverly concealed within this arcaded undercroft are a vaulted swimming pool and family theater or "media room," with access via an elevator to the master suite above. The landscape architect Charles Stick designed the dramatic garden terracing, which drops in a series of curving platforms and steps to the outside

swimming pool and rock garden below. The wider landscape design was implemented by Jody Staunton.

One of Fairfax & Sammons's great strengths is the way they can work an existing house into a significantly upgraded and enlarged design without destroying—indeed, usually enhancing—the original character. This project is a good demonstration of that skill, combining good planning and rationalization with architectural integrity.

The new accommodation on the south side is linked to the original house by a great hall with a traditionally made heavy timber king post truss roof in white oak, modeled on one in Winchester, England. This dominant space is conceived as a living hall. It has a galleried library with a spiral stair at one

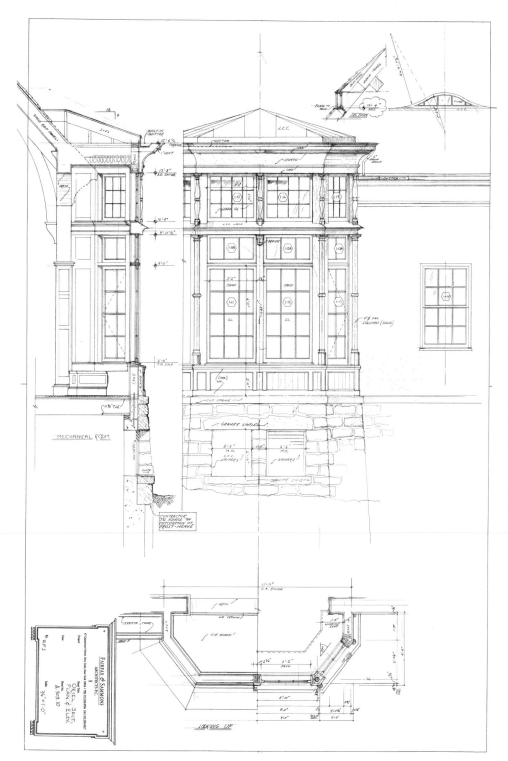

FACING PAGE *The heavily timbered living hall, with a limestone chimneypiece to the double-sided fireplace in the great central chimney stack. Beyond is the bar area, with bedroom landing above.*

LEFT *Working drawing for oriel window.*

ABOVE *Oriel window in living hall.*

end, and a double-sided fireplace with a flue rising up like a huge stone pier in the center. Conscious references to the Elizabethan hall are interpreted through an Arts and Crafts sensibility: high, limed oak wainscot paneling, molded segmental arched stone chimneypieces, and an oriel window with a ribbed ceiling. The walls are finished with limewashed plaster, against which the heavy oak trusses and purlins of the roof structure are left exposed.

Beyond the hall, in arms to south and southeast, are a study overlooking the clifflike end of the house, and a screened porch/sun room, which leads to the garden terrace. Above them is the principal bedroom and dressing room suite. Fairfax & Sammons are masters at the art of designing luxurious bedroom quarters, and this one is no exception. The millwork detail is of the highest quality, and the master bedroom, with a big gable window overlooking the lake, has charming

ABOVE *The dining room, looking out to Lake Waccabuc.*

RIGHT *The dining room, which opens through to a book-lined sitting room at one end.*

added touches, such as a ceiling shaped like an upturned keel, a high window seat beneath one of the smaller dormer windows, and a bed recess flanked by round-arched doors.

In the existing building a transverse hall has been added on the west side to create a gallery plan, with square openings through to the remodeled dining room and sitting room on the lakefront. These rooms, with their lower beamed ceilings, feel more intimate in scale; the dining room opens through to a book-lined sitting room with a fireplace at one end. A gable with a three-light window onto the lake has been added on the bedroom floor above. Fairfax & Sammons also remodeled the 1970s kitchen so that it is now expressed externally as a loggia, with a more gently sloping roof. The limewashed walls are cream-colored throughout; Ellie Cullman of Cullman & Kravis was responsible for the interior decoration.

Observant and informed visitors will appreciate Richard Sammons's knowledge of traditional detail, and his careful attention to each element of the design: the high wainscot paneling in the new transverse hall integrates with the architraves of the openings, its impost providing the springing point for the arches. The bottom two rows of paneling are detailed with a mason's wash, an Elizabethan detail.

ABOVE *Master bathroom opening onto to private balcony.*

FACING PAGE *Master bedroom, with paneled barrel-arched ceiling and window seat in dormer window.*

FOLLOWING PAGES *Vaulted indoor swimming pool built into the arcaded undercroft over steeply dropping ground at the end of the house.*

Externally, steep roofs with overhanging eaves sweeping out over the upstairs rooms, eyebrow windows peeping out from the slates, and a prominent white chimneystack are all redolent of Voysey. But the playful oriel on the entrance front is pure Richard Sammons: a "little Renaissance-style fantasy" which shows the blending of detail he so enjoys. "Elizabethan architecture is to me the most uniquely English of styles," he explains. "It is incredibly interesting, as it is a fusion between the Classical and the Gothic world, overlaying a matrix of Classical detail on Gothic proportioning."

TOP *Curving stone steps leading to the outside swimming pool and rock garden in Charles Stick's dramatic garden terracing.*

ABOVE *View of lake from entrance court.*

RIGHT *Looking up from the outside swimming pool to the new wing at the south end of the house.*

A GEORGIAN-STYLE VILLA

LITCHFIELD
WASHINGTON, CONNECTICUT, 1997

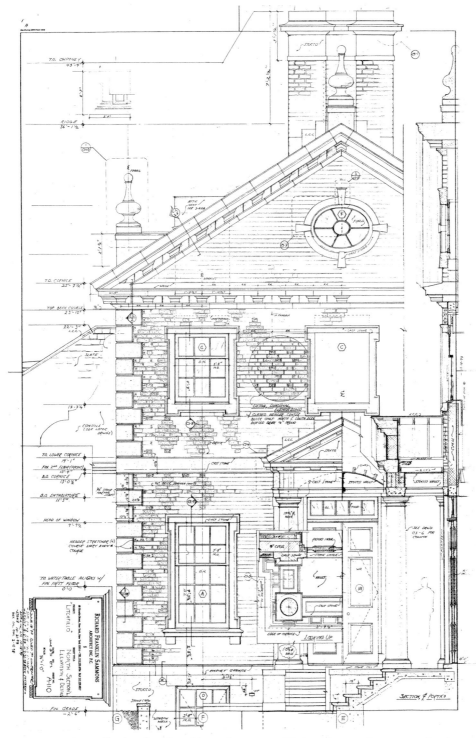

PREVIOUS PAGES *Garden elevation of house from meadow to south.*

Working drawing for entrance façade.

FACING PAGE *Entrance elevation with boxwood parterre garden designed by Peter Cummin.*

Tom Pearsall's perfect country villa was designed by Fairfax & Sammons in 1995—about the same time that they were working on nearby Lillifields for Nancy Marcantonio (page 24). Both houses reflect the influence of Jefferson—for Richard Sammons "everything goes through Jefferson"—but the contrast of moods shows how seriously

the architects take into account the different personalities of their clients.

Litchfield is the more robust of the two—a lively essay in a rustic Palladian style, with a subtle mix of restraint and late-Baroque flourishes that makes one think of the work of William Adam. Well-mannered and confident, it expresses its

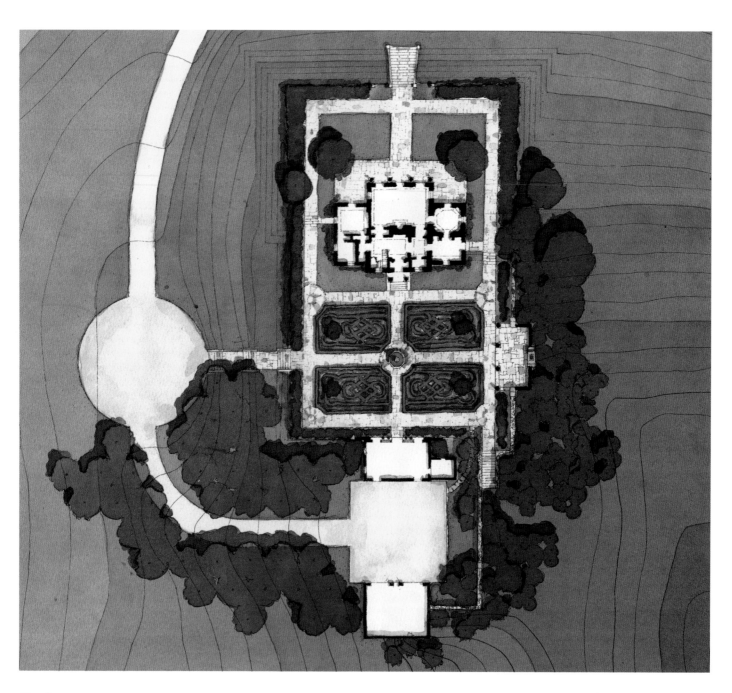

Site plan.

RIGHT *Plan of principal floor.*

FIRST FLOOR PLAN

owner's own knowledgeable interest in Classicism. It could be an Italian villa, but Richard Sammons has responded to the harsher climate of New England and the cragginess of the landscape to produce a consciously naive Palladian design that suggests the transposition of civilized architecture into a rustic setting.

The house stands on the top of a wooded hill, from which glorious views stretch south to a valley, with the hills of northwest Connecticut visible beyond. The first view of it as the mile long drive winds upwards from a brook is of the south front raised up on a terrace against the sky, a flight of stone steps leading directly down into a wild flower meadow. Solitary in this parklike setting, Litchfield gives the impression of being a folly in a designed landscape, and to this effect the architecture of its south front is more robustly detailed and Baroque in manner, the scale of its finials, volutes and freestanding columns, or standards, deliberately exaggerated.

The drive swings round to the east, so that the house is entered on its more polite north front through a garden enclosed on two sides by a Classical orangery and Tuscan columned pergola. This garden was designed by Peter Cummin, who was also responsible for the siting and wider landscaping of the house, and it reflects Litchfield's more formal face. Beside an aerial hedge of pleached hornbeam, he has made a parterre with a framework of boxwood infilled with Berberis "Crimson Pygmy," Juniperus "Blue Star" and four red crab apple trees, in the middle of which stands a handsome sundial fountain designed by Richard Sammons.

The main, three-bay temple block rises two stories over a basement (the bedroom floor reading as the attic story), flanked by slightly recessed single-story wings. On the entrance front, the basement is exposed as a granite plinth, with steps of limestone leading up to a pedimented Doric portico with a pair of eight-foot front doors. (The gradient on the other side has been raised to provide direct access to the terrace, so there is no basement drop on the south.)

Unusually for Connecticut, Litchfield is faced with brick—beautiful handmade bricks from Virginia in dark reddish browns and pinks, patterned with a rhythm of blue glazed headers. The bricks are laid in a Flemish cross bond, with a subtly interwoven diaper pattern that plays like a gentle shadow across the main block. This enlivens and enhances the wonderful surface textures that are a feature of the house, as does the "ragged" pointing, which sustains the building's vernacular character and prevents it from looking too refined. Although not widely seen in Connecticut, the detailing of the brickwork echoes that of some other houses in the neighborhood.

Crisp dressings of pale cast stone lend contrast and texture to the building. They define the architectural detail that enlivens the temple block—rusticated quoins, eared architraves, a dentil cornice with heavy block modillions, pediment finials, prominent chimney caps, and the scrolled volutes that mark the transition to the lower wings. On these wings, the sash windows have flat, gauged brick arches and only their

Stair hall with distressed limestone flagged floor

keystones are picked out in stone. The south side is partly rendered in a color to match the stone, which serves to lighten the façade and lend definition to the principal floor. On the roofs, Vermont slates are graduated in thickness, width, and exposure. This exemplifies the sound detailing and craftsmanship, and the use of good, traditional methods and materials that adds so much to the enjoyment of this house, and to its sense of solidity and robust presence in the landscape.

Litchfield is deceptively small, low in maintenance, and economical to run. It is equipped with a geothermal heating system, has a high level of insulation, and gains maximum benefit from passive solar energy. As with other Fairfax & Sammons houses, the source for its compact plan is Robert Morris's pattern book *Rural Architecture* of 1750. The main block—divided by that hallmark of the New England house, the great central chimney stack—is logically organized to accommodate the entrance hall, staircase, and powder room on one side of the hearth, the living room on the other, with the dining room and kitchen in the west wing, and a guest bedroom and bathroom

Watercolor sketch by the owner showing proposed decoration of the living room.

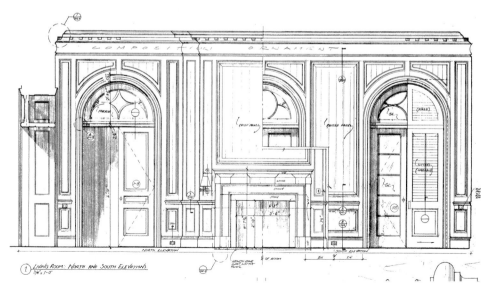

Working drawing for living room.

View of the living room.

Watercolor sketch by the owner showing proposed decoration of the dining room.

View of the octagonal dining room.

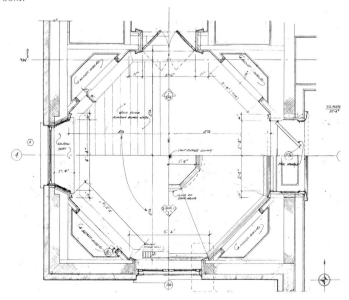

Floor plan of dining room.

PREVIOUS PAGES *The orangery and parterre garden, viewed from the guest bedroom.*

ABOVE *The parterre garden, bordered by a hedge of pleached hornbeam.*

RIGHT *The parterre garden, with limestone sundial fountain made by Texas Carved Stone to Richard Sammons's design, and fireplace framed by pergola beyond.*

in the east. The upper floor has just two ensuite bedrooms and bathrooms—one the master bedroom, with a canopy bed designed by Fairfax & Sammons. In the roof is a long open space lit by oculi in the pediments at each end.

The vestibule leads into an off-center stair hall, with the stair, as at Loxleigh (page 232), tucked unpretentiously into the northeast corner of the main block, so that it runs up across the window on the left of the front door. Flanking the fireplace on the north wall is a pair of round-arched openings inset with antiqued mirror and circular tracery transoms. They lead into the living room, which spans the full width of the central block and has three similarly round-arched French doors leading onto the terrace on the south front. These doors are designed to open outwards, allowing a double layer of inner screens—one a blind, the other a louvered shutter—to slide sideways like pocket doors into the wall space.

The status of this principal room is signified by its higher ceiling (raising the floor of the master bedroom above), and the detail of its cornice, which repeats that of the exterior, with the addition of a Grinling Gibbons-style acanthus frieze. The Carrara marble chimneypiece is a later addition by the owner—a grander replacement of the simpler original version designed by Richard Sammons. Raised paneling extends the full height of the room, its lower half treated as a dado and painted a paler color, with a faux marble skirting board.

Interconnecting with the living room on the west side is the dining room, which, like that at Lillifields, is octagonal. It has a shallow domed ceiling with a brioche top, and segmental

Working drawing for garden façade.

FACING PAGE *Detail of the garden façade, with its parade of freestanding columns.*

arched bookshelf recesses on four of its eight sides. A French door leads onto the terrace on the south front, and a window lights the west wall. To the north lies the kitchen, a smallish room neatly contained in the northwest corner of the house, with a boarded ceiling and a brick-nogged floor. Mr. Pearsall is

a perfectionist with a considerable knowledge of period design, and he has undertaken the interior decoration himself. It is an ongoing project, but he has set out his vision for the finished appearance of this exquisite villa in a series of accomplished watercolors, several of which are featured here.

A Writer's Residence
above the Hudson

Sneden's Landing
The Palisades, New York, 2004

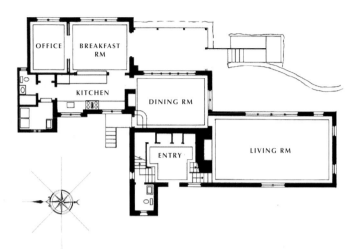

PREVIOUS PAGES *View of the main entrance framed by the eaves of the guest house.*

LEFT *Living room with view of dining room beyond.*

ABOVE *Plan of main floor.*

Such is the rustic charm of this weekend getaway, that it might be mistaken for an old farmhouse far from the city. But it is in fact just 35 minutes from Broadway, and was built as a simple weekend cottage in the 1920s. The house stands perched on the edge of that dramatic wooded scarp known as the Palisades, which overlooks the Hudson River from the west.

The present owners are Arthur Collins, a retired professor of philosophy, and his wife Linda, a fiction writer who grew up in the neighboring town. They asked Fairfax & Sammons to enlarge Sneden's Landing in a sympathetic manner to create a comfortable weekend escape from the city, and a place where they could work in peace.

The building is of a smaller scale and more modest than many of the architects' other projects, but it gave Richard Sammons the opportunity to indulge his interest in vernacular buildings that have the ring of traditional craftsmanship, in sympathy with the owners' own tastes. The Arts and Crafts spirit of the place is expressed in the bare "flag wall" masonry, the picturesque grouping of ranges of differing heights, the asymmetrical fenestration and prominent chimney stacks, and the carved front door, which is set into a round-arched opening beneath an elongated "eyebrow" canopy.

The house is entered through a gabled central block that runs back to the steeply terraced riverfront, where its walls rise from the living rock. To the right of the entrance stair hall is a barnlike range containing, on the ground floor, the living

ABOVE *Breakfast room overlooking the Hudson River. The Spanish Baroque screen has been in situ since this wing was built.*

RIGHT *The dining room, with old oak furniture from England.*

room, and in the roof space above, Linda's writing studio, which was created out of several rooms. The interiors—simply but stylishly furnished with exposed ceiling joists and lime-washed walls throughout— hint at a bohemian artist's retreat. In the upstairs studio, bare wooden floors are laid with dazzling red and blue rugs woven by Marsh Arabs in Iraq. The long, whitewashed living room has a large, unadorned fireplace at one end; an inscription, which translates from Latin as "frequent friends are the ornament of the house," is carved into the beam above. The room is sparely decorated, with contemporary paintings by friends and relatives (including the owners' son, Jacob Collins, a well-known artist), pieces of well-crafted wooden furniture, and rugs laid over bare brick floors. The brick flows out uninterrupted to merge with the paving of the riverside terrace, creating a strong visual link between the inner and outer spaces.

The central range was heightened to accommodate a master bedroom suite on the upper floor, with a balcony overlooking the Hudson. The open roof structure includes the feature of a

Guesthouse, with one of the wild peacocks that roam the garden.

RIGHT *The rear of the house, built into the escarpment of the Palisades that drops away eastwards to the Hudson River.*

large oculus in the apex of the gable, which faces east towards the river to catch the morning sun. The dining room below, with old oak furniture from England, continues the rustic theme, with a projecting chimneybreast of stepped, white-washed bricks, and a low beamed ceiling. To the north is a lower extension, with a beautiful river view. This contains the kitchen and a breakfast/sitting room and study, separated by a tall Spanish Baroque timber screen. The screen was a feature of the original house and its height dictated the ceiling level in these rooms.

In the garden, which slopes down from the road to the terraced cliff edge on which the house is sited, the architects have had fun with a former goat shed. They have converted it into a guest annex—a quaint, half-timbered eye catcher in an English Arts and Crafts style, with a pretty oculus and louvered fleche. With the help of two gardeners, Linda Collins has cultivated one acre of the garden with English-style borders filled with tulips, irises, and other plants as colorful as the neighbors' peacocks, leaving the other acre as a natural woodland setting for the house and garden.

GREENWICH VILLAGE TOWNHOUSES

Entrance hall of Italianate townhouse.

FACING PAGE *New stoops and cornices to a pair of Italianate townhouses.*

Few cities can boast a complex of historic terraced housing that has survived on such a scale as New York's Greenwich Village. For cohesiveness and quality of craftsmanship, and the contribution it makes to the urban streetscape, it is comparable to the Georgian New Town of Edinburgh in Scotland. It appeals, perhaps, because it is built to a human scale. In recent years, this enclave of tree-shaded streets lined with elegant facades of warm brown brick or stone has undergone a renaissance, and more and more of its houses are now being converted back to single occupancy and sympathetically restored. Fairfax & Sammons has made a significant contribution to this revival, with many restoration schemes of exemplary quality.

Among the examples featured here are representatives of each of the main architectural styles that characterize the Village, from Federal and Greek Revival, to Anglo-Italianate. Greek Revival townhouses typically followed pattern books such as those published by Minard Lafever and Asher Benjamin, American architects active in the early nineteenth century. The use of Greek forms had been introduced in the previous century by the book *The Antiquities of Athens* by Stuart and Revett, and it traveled across to America. The Greek Revival style is pivotal in being both the last gasp of the Renaissance and the first style of the Romantic Movement. Its simplicity of form appealed to the Calvinistic nature of the American public and the speculative builder of the time. Decorative elements were easily fashioned out of timber and simply run plaster, although they could also be highly carved and ornamented. The Italianate style that followed was typified by larger, deeper, and more vertically proportioned houses, with details that were no longer flat, broad, and spare, but rather more robust. It represented a somewhat confused amalgam of Renaissance forms—enough to be considered "Italian" in style, yet unlike any building seen in Italy.

Fairfax & Sammons have tackled the problems inherent in the building type, such as constraints of size, insensitive subdivisions, and the gradual erosion of defining architectural ornament, with care and ingenuity, supported by their knowledgeable understanding of the genre and conscientious historic research. Employing materials and craftsmen of the highest quality, they have set a high standard of design and workmanship that emulates the work of the master masons and carpenters who built the houses in the early and mid-nineteenth century.

In comparison to Fairfax & Sammons's other work, these townhouse projects are relatively small scale—the "bread and butter" of the practice, as it were. But in the context of revitalizing a designated historic district, their significance is considerable.

THE ENTRANCE

New York's historic townhouses are still used in very much the same way as they were in the nineteenth century. Their principal public rooms have generally remained on the original parlor floor, raised-up above the noise of street level. Many entrances are reached by climbing a stoop—a feature dating back to the days of New Amsterdam which Fairfax & Sammons has had much experience in restoring. The architects have also reinstated many lost stoops.

Once inside, a townhouse tends to become more ornate. The vestibule, which serves both as a weather break and as a transition from public to private spaces, typically features highly polished painted wood paneling, with the stairs figuring prominently in the narrow plan. Every opportunity is taken to exploit design possibilities.

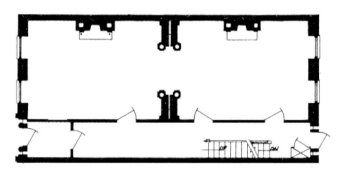

ABOVE *Typical townhouse floor plan showing entrance hall and double parlors.*

ABOVE LEFT *An Italianate townhouse entrance and stair hall, with a restored encaustic tile floor in the vestibule and new reclaimed wood floor in the stair hall beyond.*

LEFT *Detail of newly replaced vestibule doors, showing prominent moldings typical of the Anglo-Italianate style.*

FACING PAGE *A new hand-carved staircase in a Greek Revival townhouse on Jane Street, with a walnut newel post carved as a scrolled volute by master craftsman, John Desario. The design was based on an example documented in the* Historic American Building Survey.

THE PARLOR FLOOR

The restoration of the main, or parlor, floor of a town-house often involves such tasks as replicating plaster moldings, locating salvaged chimneypieces of the period, and restoring gilded pier mirrors, such as the one shown on the left. Typically, townhouse owners want all of the original detail restored or reinstated, as well as new amenities, such as air conditioning and audio systems, installed throughout. Fairfax & Sammons cleverly work new systems and storage space (which was almost non-existant in nineteenth-century houses), into an existing plan without destroying the character and scale of the original interior. Their restoration work is underpinned by a scholarly knowledge of historic styles and associated moldings, combined with the careful study of surviving precedents.

ABOVE *The restored parlor floor of a small Greek Revival townhouse on West 4th Street, with new moldings based on Minard Lafever's designs published in* The Modern Builders Guide *of 1833. Note the storage closets worked into the walls between the dining and living rooms.*

FACING PAGE *Living room in an Italianate townhouse of the 1860s. The tall, double-hung sash windows have internal shutters—a typical feature of New York townhouses of all periods since their façades are often too narrow to accommodate external ones. Here, the sash windows have been designed to look like casements, a clever conceit achieved by introducing a broad, beaded central mullion. The owner found the period Carrara marble chimneypiece in New Orleans. The pier mirror between the windows has been stripped of its white paint and re-gilded.*

FOLLOWING PAGES *The restored parlor of an Italianate townhouse, featuring characteristic tall doors and an original marble chimneypiece.*

THE DINING ROOM

The Greenwich Village townhouse often incorporated both a main formal dining room on the parlor floor, and a more intimate family dining room on the ground floor, for use on a more regular, informal basis.

ABOVE *A restored ground floor dining room occupying the front of an Italianate townhouse, where originally the family dining room would have been.*

FACING PAGE *A parlor floor breakfast room in a new addition to a Greek Revival townhouse, with south-facing windows overlooking the newly restored garden. This room is adjacent to a small kitchen, which has been cleverly tucked into a bay behind the stairs. The opening in the brick wall on the right leads into the formal dining room.*

THE KITCHEN

Houses renovated to suit the needs of modern family life often focus strongly on the kitchen. Whether the new kitchen in a Greenwich Village townhouse is located on the ground floor at the rear, as was typical in the nineteenth century, or on the parlor floor, most now feature the latest conveniences and technology.

FACING PAGE *A new galley-type kitchen fitted into one bay of a Greek Revival townhouse, with stone work surfaces and a flagged floor.*

ABOVE *A new scullery, serving double duty as a butler's pantry and informal bar. Simple bead-boarded paneling and painted cabinets complement the farmhouse sink.*

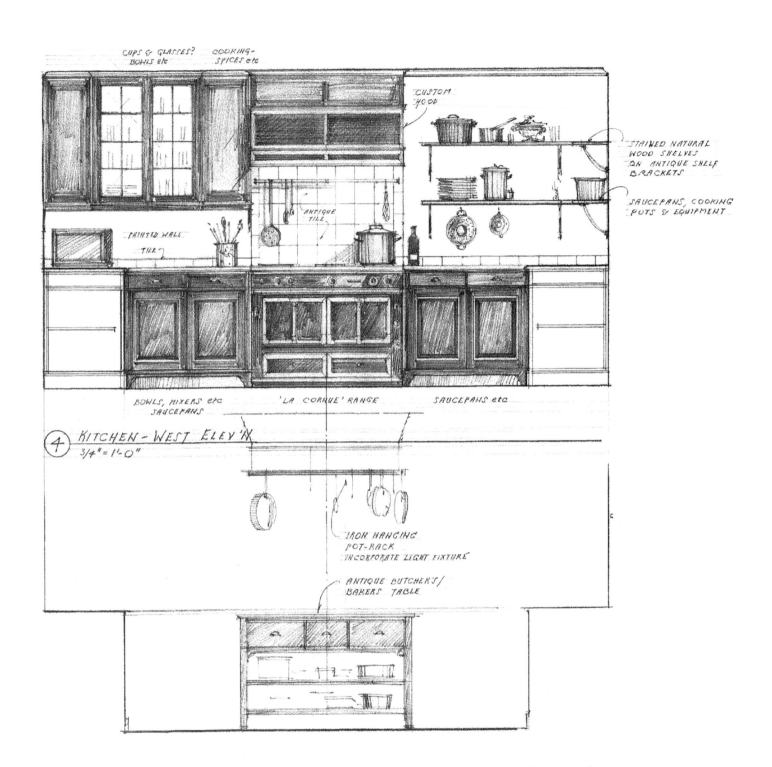

CUPS & GLASSES? COOKING-
BOWLS etc SPICES etc

CUSTOM HOOD

STAINED NATURAL
WOOD SHELVES
ON ANTIQUE SHELF
BRACKETS

SAUCEPANS, COOKING
POTS & EQUIPMENT

ANTIQUE TILE

PAINTED WALL
TILE?

BOWLS, MIXERS etc
SAUCEPANS

'LA CORNUE' RANGE

SAUCEPANS etc

④ KITCHEN - WEST ELEV'N
3/4" = 1'-0"

IRON HANGING
POT-RACK
INCORPORATE LIGHT FIXTURE

ANTIQUE BUTCHER'S/
BAKERS TABLE

A conceptual drawing for the kitchen featured opposite.

FACING PAGE *Worktops of Carrara marble
contrast crisply with black painted cupboards
in this ground floor kitchen, which opens
directly onto a garden at the rear. The open
shelving and reclaimed pine floor emphasize
the informal nature of this kitchen.*

THE MASTER BEDROOM SUITE

O ften a major element of a townhouse renovation is the owner's desire for a master bedroom suite with good-sized bedroom and bathroom, and the generous pro-vision of storage closets. In most cases, these requirements result in the master bedroom suite occupying an entire floor. Fairfax & Sammons's great skill is demonstrated in the way it can balance the aesthetic considerations of a historic building with the practical needs of a typical modern lifestyle.

FACING PAGE *One solution, for a busy two-career family, was to install the master bathroom across the entire front room of their Italianate townhouse. The chimneypiece, moldings and wooden floor are all original features, carefully restored by the architects.*

ABOVE RIGHT *A master bedroom suite in an 1830s Greek Revival townhouse, with an interconnecting sitting room (seen in the fore-ground) and a view to the rear over a quiet garden. Simple crown moldings are an appropriate complement to contemporary furnish-ings provided by the decorator, Thom Filicia.*

RIGHT *A generous, traditional-looking bathtub sits in the light-filled master bathroom of this Italianate townhouse.*

An ornate Eastlake mirror in an Italianate town-house, original to the house and now carefully restored. Historically, this was called a pier glass, since it was designed to hang against the pier between two tall windows in order to provide the illusion of another window.

FACING PAGE Situated on a prominent corner site, this is a particularly fine example of a brick townhouse dating from 1860s. The façade is emphatically Italianate—vertical in proportion, with a high base-ment and tall sash windows. The decorative cast iron railings running along the street and up the front steps are replica replacements of the originals. All these details were based on surviving evidence of the nineteenth-century work.

A CITY APARTMENT

PARK AVENUE
NEW YORK, NEW YORK, 1996

The great skill of the two firms that collaborated on this project—the architects, Fairfax & Sammons, and the interior designers, Mlinaric, Henry and Zervudachi Ltd.—is their ability to engage with and understand owners such as these clients—an intellectual couple with an extensive knowledge of the arts, a passion for books, and highly cultivated tastes. In addition to providing this sixth-floor Park Avenue apartment with a series of smart, elegant rooms for entertaining, they had to incorporate into it a private retreat for contemplative study. The skill with which they achieved this, interpreting their clients' needs to create a suitably architectural setting for their sophisticated lifestyle and academic interests, is all the more impressive given the spatial constraints and limited outlook that this 5,000-square-foot apartment presented.

Fairfax & Sammons completely reconfigured it, remodeling every space and renewing every fitting. The architecture and decoration of the principal rooms has a strong Soanian theme, which is enhanced by Anglo-French detailing in the style of Thomas Hope, and furniture and antiques of the period bought for the apartment by David Mlinaric and Hugh Henry.

The principal rooms open off a Neoclassical entrance hall, which was designed as a rotunda, with a shallow dome coaxed out of the flat painted ceiling. The walls, inset with marble reliefs by Thorvaldsen, are painted and lined out to imitate ashlar. English Empire style chairs combine effectively with a rug and light fitting of the 1930s.

One of the principal features of this apartment is the way it was conceived as a home for a remarkable collection of books. In addition to a Neoclassical library, bookshelves are integrated into the dining room, which doubles as a library,

The Soanian dining room, with a copy of the antique chimneypiece in the drawing room. The roundels above the bookshelves were modeled by Anthony Visco.

FACING PAGE *Library with shallow Soanian cross-vault and exedra end. The chairs are early-nineteenth-century Greek Revival.*

and into the walls of the study. The Soane-inspired library is ingeniously fitted into an unlit space beside the master bedroom suite. It is cross-vaulted with an apsidal end, and intricately fitted out with quarter-sawn maple and ebonized paneling and bookshelves containing numerous secret spaces and cupboards. Georgian green panels combine with blue painted bookshelves to give the room its beautiful peacock colors. Appropriate furniture and antiques, such as the set of early-nineteenth-century Greek Revival chairs with friezes on their top rails, and the bust displayed in the apse, were bought by Mr. Mlinaric in England.

In the drawing room, the walls are painted a mustard color and the floor laid with oak parquet de Versailles, a feature of the original apartment. A huge rug from the New York dealer Nader Bolour provides a rich background for the plushly-upholstered chairs and other furnishings. The English eighteenth-century marble chimneypiece is by Henry Holland; an exact copy was made for the interconnecting dining room.

Fairfax & Sammons worked closely with David Mlinaric and Hugh Henry on all the details of this project, from the design of plaster moldings to the color of each element, with additional significant input from the clients. The result of this informed, coordinated vision is most impressive in the dining room—a masterful transformation from a tight, rear space with no outlook into one of the most unusual and architectural dining rooms in New York. The solution was to create enough interest around the walls to turn the room inwards, articulating the space with Soanian recesses inset with mirrors, with bookshelves integrated into their pilasters and dados. So often, smart dining rooms possess a somewhat chilly air, but here the incorporation of books makes the room feel comfortable and well used. The striking Pompeian color scheme, which was inspired by the chimneypiece's porphyry slips, is picked up in the colors of the rug and reflected in the antiqued mirrors; it gives the room a warmth and richness that is particularly alluring by candlelight. Set into the walls above the pilaster bookcases are roundels modeled by Anthony Visco of Philadelphia. They depict busts of U.S. presidents and other worthies, as featured on dollar notes. The room is hung with mostly English eighteenth-century portraits collected by the owner, and an Empire-style gilt bronze chandelier.

The private quarters are suitably opulent, with a Napoleonic-style master bathroom paneled in mahogany, and extensive dressing rooms. The female quarters include an office, generous provision of powder blue paneled and mirrored cupboards, and even a circular sable closet. Beautifully made cabinets and vanity units repeat the fluted and elliptical forms of other details in the apartment. These photographs constitute a unique record of Fairfax & Sammons's grandest city commission. Since they were taken the apartment has been sold, but it is described here as it appeared until recently.

Master bedroom.

RIGHT *Dressing table.*

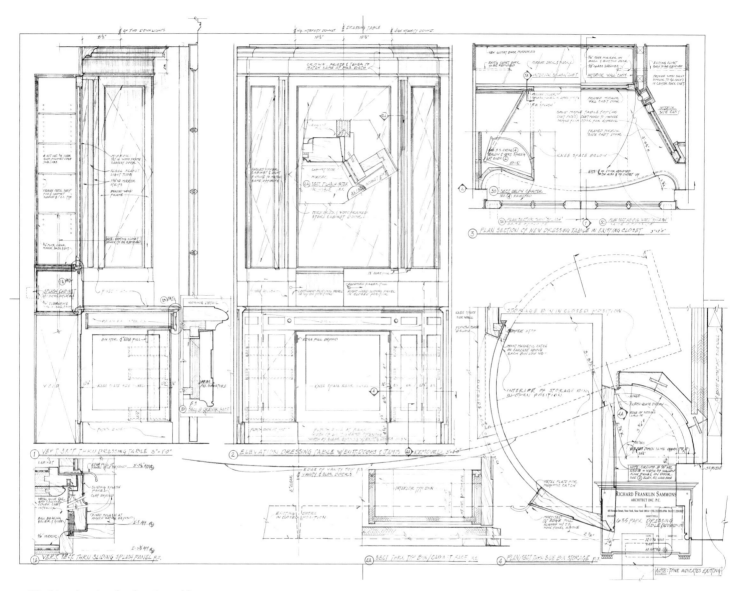

Working drawing for dressing table.

A LIBRARY ON CENTRAL PARK

THE GAINSBOROUGH STUDIOS
NEW YORK, NEW YORK, 1996

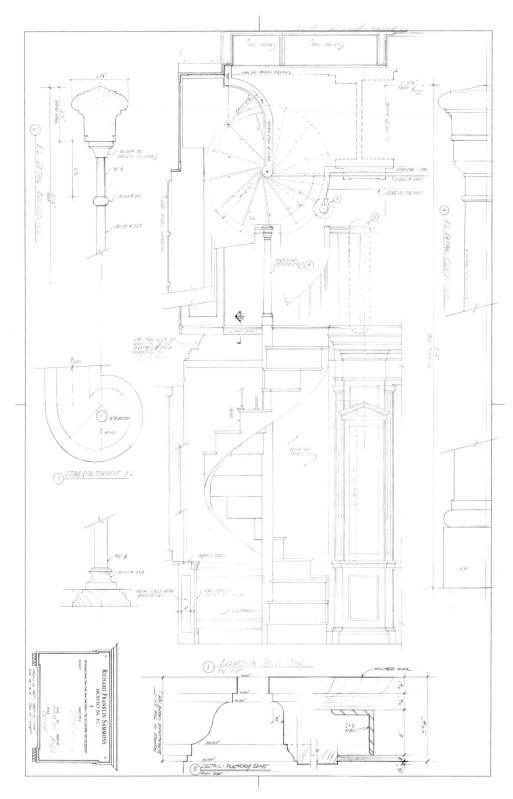

PREVIOUS PAGES *Library sitting room overlooking Central Park.*

ABOVE *Working drawing for library stair.*

FACING PAGE *Spiral stair of maple wood modeled on a stair in the Chapel of San Lorenzo in Santa Fe.*

In 1996 Donald Oresman, a retired corporate lawyer, presented Fairfax & Sammons with a direct but challenging brief: he wanted the main space of his Manhattan apartment—a narrow, double-height former artist's studio overlooking Central Park—transformed as a Renaissance-style library.

Having rejected a scheme by Richard Meier, he approached Richard Sammons on the recommendation of a friend whose library Fairfax & Sammons also designed. Mr. Oresman wanted a library that could provide maximum storage and display space for a most unusual collection. In addition to accommo-

Portfolio storage under staircase.

FACING PAGE *Study space/bird-watching perch overlooking Central Park, balancing the spiral staircase on the opposite side of the room.*

dating some 2,000 volumes of mostly literary criticism, contemporary fiction, and poetry—a mere fifth of a collection, the larger part of which resides in his country house at Larchmont on Long Island Sound—it had to house the core of a unique body of about 1,800 works of art, each of which depicts a person or group of people reading.

In Richard Sammons, Mr. Oresman found an architect sympathetic to his literary and artistic tastes, who could design a suitably uplifting setting without losing sight of practicalities. The client's sole instruction was that his new library should be created using a light wood rather than the more traditional mahogany or dark-stained oak, since the studio apartment is lit only by northern light.

The result is a miniature Renaissance-style library of French polished maple wood, beautifully detailed and fitted out with pediment-ended bookcases. These project at right angles into the room to create a series of bays beneath a heavily coffered ceiling. Compact and intimate, the library doubles as a living room, with comfortable sofas in the center and a dining/meeting area at one end, beyond which are a small kitchen, bathroom and sitting room. Mezzanine galleries above the bookcases accommodate more shelving and provide access to a balustraded sleeping balcony over the dining area.

The room's fluid lines reach their climax in the spiral staircase—a delightfully graceful twist of maple wood with thin metal balusters that takes as its model a similar structure in the Chapel of San Lorenzo at Santa Fe, New Mexico. Balancing it on the opposite side of the window is a circular study space which projects like a pulpit from the end of the west gallery. The fireplace in the central bay has had its opening narrowed to suit the new proportions of the room. It is fitted with a timber chimneypiece painted black to resemble marble, and on its

hearth stone a motto has been inscribed by the English master carver Simon Verity, reading: "Try Again, Fail Again, Fail Better."

The mezzanine floor was reconfigured to open out the bed space, which is flanked by mirrored cupboard doors, bowed to echo the curve of the balcony. These, together with mirrored panels on the side walls, give the room the impression of a rotunda, and help to counteract the somewhat telescopic effect that such a tall, narrow space creates with only one outside view.

It is, however, a magnificent view—a long, north facing sweep over the tree tops of Central Park from the sixth floor of Gainsborough Studios, a narrow, steel framed block of studio apartments built in 1905 to the design of Charles W. Buckham. A dramatic window opening fills the apartment's whole north wall, broken across its center by a pedimented blind window and architrave. This is an existing feature which has been retained, as has the staircase beside the entrance to the apartment. Formerly both of dark wood, they have been painted in faux maple to match the new joinery.

Mr. Oresman compares his passion for collecting to Captain Ahab's single-minded pursuit of Moby Dick: "There's a certain Ahabian monomania about me: once I started, I became pretty relentless," he says. The seed of the collection was a large picture by Jim Dine called *Nancy Reading*, which he and his wife, Patricia, saw in a gallery one day when they were newly married. "We collected contemporary art and we both liked it very much, so we bought it," says Mr. Oresman. "A few weeks later, in a different gallery, we saw another large portrait—this time of the poet Frank O'Hara reading at a desk in a river of his own words. Since I have a kind of file clerk mentality, I suggested that, rather than buying from time to time just what we liked, it might be fun to start collecting readers. That was 20 years ago."

The range of material is astonishing: there are readers here in every conceivable media, ranging from pen-and-ink drawings and cartoons, gouaches, prints, lithographs, photographs, watercolors, oils, and acrylics to works in needlepoint, painted leather strips and ceramics. Sculptures include conventional bronze, stone and cast iron pieces, as well as creations in plastic, papier mâché, and glass, and there are even some made of balsa wood, light bulbs, and scrap metal.

Mr. Oresman says that he is not trying to shape the collection to a particular vision, but rather to establish what the past

century has had to say about people reading (he buys nothing pre-1900). Few are abstract, but his explanation for this is that "art that is anti-intellectual is unlikely to be about reading"; Cubism is about as abstract as he gets. But the collection, which now runs to an 11-volume catalogue, is unconstrained by geographical boundaries; it includes works from South America and Japan, although about 95 percent is American or European. "It's the image I'm interested in—period," he says. "I don't care whether it's by a famous or an unknown artist, all I care about is the image."

The list of names in the former category is certainly impressive: Picasso, Matisse, Giacometti, Cocteau, Chagall, Leger, Balthus, Diego Rivera, Gwen John, Aubrey Beardsley, Max Beerbohm, Roger Fry, Eric Gill, Duncan Grant, Vanessa Bell, and Henry Moore all feature. Among American artists are well-known names such as Thomas Hart Benton and Reginald Marsh, and many from the famous Ashcan School active around the turn of last century. The "unknowns" range from Depression-era artists to contemporary students. "Photographs have to be fairly adventurous to interest me, otherwise they're verging on journalism," Mr. Oresman says, citing Bernice Abbot and Henri Cartier-Bresson as among those whose work features in the collection.

About 300 works are displayed on walls and other surfaces in the library room and an adjacent apartment, which Mr. Oresman also owns. Some hang on hinged wall panels that open out, others on sliding panels designed to reveal the pictures in successive layers. Many are stored in built-in portfolio drawers under the stairs, or in boxes secreted in cupboards beneath the bookshelves. Each surface is carefully articulated with well-proportioned Classical detail, the pedimented faces of the bookcases modeled on ancient tabernacles, which held precious scrolls. Having them project at right angles to the room resolves the fact that books and pictures do not complement each other when viewed on the same plane; it also doubles the shelf space.

Although he owns houses in Westchester County and Vermont, Mr. Oresman prefers to spend most of his time in this library home at the heart of his native city. What could be more inspiring for a bibliophile collector than to sit in this serene space, looking out over the long, green canyon of Central Park, surrounded by books and in the company of hundreds of silent, carefully chosen reading companions?

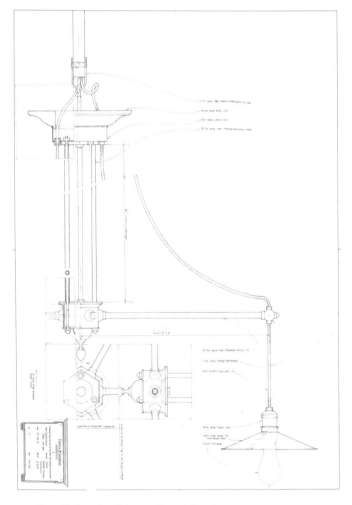

An Arts and Crafts Manhattan Studio for a Composer

NEW YORK, NEW YORK, 2000

It is appropriate that the distinguished Classical composer, Stefania de Kenessey, should have chosen this ground floor apartment as her working studio and arts salon, since it is one of the original double-height studio apartments created on West 67th Street between 1903 and 1919, according to an idea conceived by the artist Henry W. Ranger. It occupies the earliest of six "grand and distinctive" cooperative apartment buildings—a loosely Jacobethan block dating from 1903 which was probably designed by George Mort Pollard, architect of the most famous building in the enclave, the Hotel des Artistes. The area is still popular with artists and musicians today.

When Stefania de Kenessey commissioned Fairfax & Sammons to remodel the apartment they had already become friends, having met through an arts organization she had begun. For architects who are used to working in tandem with smart interior decorators, she had an unusual request: she asked them not only to remodel the architectural elements of the interior, but also to buy or design all the furniture and fittings and to mastermind the redecoration. "Luckily I know their taste well enough to trust it," she says, "I knew we were in aesthetic sympathy." The project was a rare opportunity for Fairfax & Sammons to carry their vision right through to the last detail of the furnishings. The result, which is inspired by the architectural tenor of the whole building and the creative impetus that inspired the concept, demonstrates well the architects' ability to design fluently in a manner that revives the original Arts and Crafts spirit of the place. It possesses a satisfactory sense of continuity.

The apartment is dominated by the tall, north-facing studio space that retains its original jack-arched ceiling. Three interconnecting vaulted spaces—dining room and sitting room/library, with kitchen beyond—open off it to the south. Above them, on a mezzanine floor, are sleeping quarters and an office. Fairfax & Sammons made several small alterations to the plan, but they completely redesigned the internal finishes, with the notion that the studio would function both as a music studio for the owner and as a venue for salon functions organized by the Derriere Guard.

The treatment of the studio room was inspired by a photograph of the interior of Kildowie in Maidenhead, England, by Dunn and Watson, which shows a room also dominated by a large window with a window seat at its base and with a gallery around one side. In the de Kenessey apartment, the tall mullioned and transomed studio window, which has its original diamond-paned leaded lights, provides a backdrop to the composer's Steinway grand piano, the main focus of the room. Simple stile and rail wainscot paneling and a new chimney-

TOP *Detail of studio chimneypiece and wainscot.*

ABOVE *Working drawing for chandelier.*

FACING PAGE *Studio room/salon, hung with an exhibition of works by the artist Jacob Collins.*

LEFT *Studio/salon looking toward the north-facing courtyard window.*

ABOVE *Entrance hall with oak settle designed by Sir Edwin Lutyens and sculpture by Frederick Hart.*

piece take their cue from the English Arts and Crafts architect C. F. A. Voysey, while the brass chandeliers—also designed by Fairfax & Sammons—were modelled on an original of the period seen in London. Pale Farrow and Ball paints were chosen for the studio to induce a suitably calm mood; this neutral palette also provides a backdrop for the display of a changing exhibition of paintings and architectural renderings associated with the Derriere Guard. The only feature not replaced was the open staircase, which ascends on the south wall to a gallery landing.

The entrance hall was also paneled in American white oak, but stained dark rather than painted, and with a William Morris wallpaper above the dado. This provides an appropriate context for an oak settle designed by Sir Edwin Lutyens as part of the original furnishings of the Drum Inn at Cockington near Torquay in England, of 1934. Anne Fairfax and Ben Pentreath, former head of the decoration division of Fairfax & Sammons, found this, along with other Arts and Crafts pieces, such as the beautiful curtain fabric of about 1880 that hangs between the salon and dining room, as the result of making a

LEFT *Dining room.*

ABOVE *Side table in dining room with painting by Jacob Collins.*

special trip to Britain. Indeed, the good old oak furniture collected for this project informed a lot of the architectural detail. For example, the window seat in the dining room adopts the same shallow cyma molding as the large Heals chest that was acquired for this room and serves as a sideboard.

An opening formerly existed between the dining and sitting rooms, but Anne Fairfax, with an acute architectural eye, saw a need for the suggestion of a physical distinction between the two spaces, and inserted a beam between them. The sitting room is lined with bookshelves to give the intimate feeling of a small library.

Fairfax & Sammons have responded well to the owner's brief: "I wanted something that had an elegance and simplicity to it, but also felt like a place where you could live," says Stefania de Kenessey. "Elegant, yet casual is the right combination for my taste." Anne Fairfax felt very conscious of the Café des Artistes ethos of this place, so it is appropriate that the apartment is used not only for composing music, but also as a salon, and a clubhouse for the Derriere Guard, the traditional arts and music organization founded by its owner.

An Artist's Studio Residence

Water Street Atelier on East 69th Street New York, New York, 2003

FACING PAGE *Restored façade of carriage house.*

BELOW *Old photograph showing the Water Street carriage house circa 1940.*

BOTTOM *Floor plans.*

This handsome Georgian-style former carriage house still reads as such from the street front, with large double doors flanked by single entrances beneath two floors of sash windows and a heavy modillion cornice. Dating from the early twentieth century, it had been converted into a sculpture studio, which closed in 2001. The building was left in a semi-industrial state, needing to be totally gutted for residential use.

It was acquired in 2001 by Jacob Collins and Ann Brashares, a successful Classical artist and prominent "tweens" author with a young family. They employed Fairfax & Sammons to convert the building into their family home, retaining the ground floor as an artist's studio. (The architects subsequently went on to remodel Jacob's parents' weekend residence in Sneden's Landing, New York, see page 102).

The plan is long and narrow, typical of the New York townhouse type, but it has the advantage of an exposure on all four sides, on several levels. Although the budget was not large, the architects and owners had the joint vision to do something quite dramatic. So they cut out a large section of the concrete upper floors (which had been part of the sculpture studio) to create an airy, double-height atrium. This is reached from the ground floor by an existing stair, which leads up from the entrance lobby on the right of the studio. The atrium serves as a stair hall and central space at the heart of the house; it is here that the owners have their grand piano, and the walls are used as a gallery for many of Jacob's paintings. The space is wonderfully lit, thanks to the insertion of a skylight overhead and a new large, leaded glass window on the west wall over the stair.

At the front of the building on this floor is the living room/library in a pleasantly proportioned Georgian-style room with sash windows and a robust, bolection molded wooden chimneypiece. Ben Pentreath, who headed up the decoration division, took the lead and sourced all the furniture and fabrics for this project. He also organized the upholstery and other elements of the interior decoration. The style of the furnishings is quietly traditional with a creative edge. A pale palette is used for the walls and curtains to provide a calm backdrop for the more strongly colored and boldly patterned textiles and oriental rugs that give the rooms their eclectic, richly textured feel.

To the rear of the main floor is an open plan kitchen/family dining room leading onto a large terrace. One original feature that has been preserved, and which adds greatly to the appearance of the dining area, is the heavily beamed ceiling covered

2ND FLOOR

3RD FLOOR

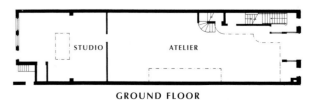

GROUND FLOOR

View of staircase and landing balcony, which wrap around the central atrium.

FACING PAGE *Central stairhall atrium looking toward kitchen.*

in decorative tinwork. Good old furniture bought specially in London, combined with kilim rugs on wooden floor boards, paintings by Jacob Collins, and the architects' trademark kitchen fittings, create a room that is understated rather than ostentatious, reflecting the style of its owners. Completed within the constraints of an extremely strict budget, this project shows how effective the intelligent use of stock catalog moldings can be when combined with an inventive yet subtle eye.

The main staircase leads up from the central hall to a balustraded gallery landing on the bedroom floor. Above this is a small penthouse apartment with a rooftop garden and writing room. (Ann Brashares has recently become one of the country's most successful authors, with her best-seller, *Sisterhood of the Travelling Pants*, recently made into a very successful movie.) At street level, the carriage doors lead directly into the studio, which has been kept very much as found and preserves wonderfully the atmosphere of a working atelier. Plaster casts and paintings are arranged around the walls; easels and all the paraphernalia of young artists at work fill the room. It is a perfect setting for the well-known art school that Jacob Collins founded at his former studio on Water Street in Brooklyn, and which he continues to run here to high regard.

LEFT *Kitchen.*

ABOVE *Dining area of kitchen with portraits by the owner, Jacob Collins*

A FORMER STABLE AND STUDIO

183 AND 185 WEST 4TH STREET IN GREENWICH VILLAGE NEW YORK, NEW YORK, 2003

Anybody familiar with the heart of Greenwich Village may have noticed on West 4th Street, between Jones and Bedford Streets, a pair of low, red brick buildings standing serene and slightly aloof amidst the boutiques and tattoo parlors that dominate this still rough-edged quarter of the Village. This is the home of Anne Fairfax and Richard Sammons, an intriguing building which started life as two—a stable/carriage house (the lefthand part) and a sculpture studio (on the right). Later remodeled as one residence, it reads from the street as a pair of polite, three-bay Georgian houses.

The lower building on the left is the earlier of the two, built sometime round the 1880s as a stable for the house behind. In 1917, it was converted into a Colonial Revival-style residence by the architect Fayerweather, and occupied by the society landscape architect Annette Hoyt Flanders. The taller righthand building, with an elegant elliptical-arched fanlight and tall casement windows, dates from 1919. It is appropriate that it started life as a sculpture studio, since at the time this area was high bohemia. The original use is evident on the interior, where the principal space is a large, double-height room lit generously on the north (rear) side. Originally occupied by an Italian sculptor, the designer of the Pierce Arrow hood ornament, it was acquired in the 1920s by the industrialist and art collector Armand Hammer, who joined the two buildings together and remodeled them as his New York home.

The unusual, somewhat quirky character of 183-5 West 4th Street, particularly apparent on the inside, is appropriate and perhaps largely due to, the succession of artistic-minded owners who over the years have responded imaginatively to the building's unconventional wedge shape and contrasts of scale. When Anne Fairfax and Richard Sammons bought the property in 2000, they embarked on a total renovation that included cleverly remodeling the interior to disguise the irregular form without destroying its idiosyncratic character.

Carefully, they repaired and reinstated the historic fabric, making subtle additions such as shutters (painted, along with the front doors, an elegant dark green) to enhance the street front. The mansard roof, which dates from 1936, is newly crested with a Chippendale-style balustrade, which echoes the cast iron grilles of the metope windows.

FACING PAGE *Living hall overlooking the garden terrace. The new limestone chimneypiece was modeled on a design by Lutyens.*

TOP *Mirrored diptych over chimneypiece in kitchen/breakfast room.*

ABOVE *Floor plans.*

transition between the quiet, domestic facade and the busy street on its doorstep. To the rear, the architects transformed a scruffy yard floored with grey industrial tiles into a pretty garden terrace with herringbone paving of handmade Virginia bricks. Accessed from both the kitchen and the living hall, this garden terrace assumes the role of an extra room. Its enclosing painted cedar wall is Classically detailed to mirror the interior, and there is an awning that can be pulled down over the entire space.

The remodeled interior makes a feature of the dramatic juxtapositions of scale. From the everyday entrance (the lefthand front door), one enters through a tiny lobby into a cozy kitchen-cum-sitting/eating room, with a low-beamed ceiling and bead-boarded walls. Conforming to the tight scale of this side of the house, a dogleg stair leads straight up from the kitchen to the owners' bedroom quarters on the attic floor above. But from the other side of this miniature kitchen/living room, one passes directly into an imposing, grandly scaled room—the former studio, remodeled as a Lutyens-style living hall. Although the street front gives no hint of it, this room occupies virtually the entire space of the righthand building, with mezzanine landings wrapped round three sides to provide access to the master bedroom quarters in the lower building, and to the guest bedroom and bathroom in the triangular shaped space overlooking the street.

The living hall demonstrates admirably Richard Sammons's and Anne Fairfax's ability to create a sense of Classical proportion and order from even the most difficult of spaces, and to achieve this with a certain wit. By introducing a bowed partition to the entrance end of the room, they have made it symmetrical, creating hidden spaces on each side which accommodate a bar and boiler room. The entire back wall has been opened up with new glazing on both levels, with the staircase repositioned to run up in front of it to the mezzanine landing above. The room's arch motif—seen in the recess over the fireplace, and in the full height arched opening framing the rear landing and glazed wall—is a direct quote from the architecture of Norman Shaw. The main arch springs from the level of the landing banister rail, which also marks the line of the dado paneling at this end of the room. The style of this paneling is in keeping with that of the great limestone chimneypiece, which was modeled on one by Lutyens at the British School in Rome. Daylight floods down through the remodeled multipaned roof light onto a floor made of quarter-sawn American white oak, waxed and tung-oiled in the traditional manner to create a lustrous backdrop for carefully chosen pieces of antique furniture.

FACING PAGE *The living hall: view from dining alcove into kitchen/bar.*

The "Black Pearl" bar.

By way of light relief after this handsome, unexpectedly grand Classical room, the space to the right of the entrance contains a consciously tongue-in-cheek bar/surrogate kitchen, with a theme that recognizes Anne Fairfax's Hawaiian upbringing. Lined with black painted paneling, and with a mahogany bar, it is called the "Black Pearl" and decorated with appropriate references to the South Seas, such as a portrait of Captain Cook, whaling voyage maps and views of Honolulu and Hawaii, ship oil lamps, and a barometer.

The contrast between the bar and the kitchen/living room is delicious, the latter possessing the air of a pretty parlor. Pale yellow walls, with architectural detail and kitchen fittings picked out in white, combine with the blue and white palette of the Delft fireplace tiles, china plates on the walls, and checked and striped loose covers over a pair of diminutive arm chairs, to give the room its very feminine air. The handsome

chimneypiece has a twin-arched overmantle fitted with mirrors, which creates an added sense of depth and contributes an architectural focus to the room, as if to anticipate the architecturally more formal space beyond.

Only by looking at the plan of the house is it possible to appreciate fully the skill with which the architects have rationalized the irregular-shaped spaces. Classically detailed partition walls adjust the proportions of a room, and clever use has been made of spaces squeezed into angles for closets, powder room and other storage.

To the unsleeping street outside, the serene presence of 183-5 West 4th Street is anathema. So unobtrusive is its double-fronted façade that it would not occur to most pedestrians to stop and give it a second thought. There is little to hint that behind the low brick walls lies one of the more interesting architectural spaces in the Village.

163

FACING PAGE *Kitchen.*

ABOVE *Master bedroom with nineteenth-century canopy bed from Virginia.*

An Upper West Side Apartment

THE PRASADA
ON CENTRAL PARK WEST
NEW YORK, NEW YORK, 2005

Façade of the Prasada Apartments on Central Park West.

RIGHT *Living room with Louis XVI-style chimneypiece.*

Entrance hall.

FACING PAGE *Bed alcove in office/guestroom.*

Occupying a prime position on the west side of Central Park, the Prasada is one of the earliest apartment blocks of its type—an imposing Beaux Arts-style building dating from 1907. This apartment had been owned and occupied by the same family for three generations when the present owner bought it, and much of its original early-twentieth-century character had been preserved. But the maid's bedroom and large kitchen were unsuited to the new owner's more contemporary lifestyle, and Fairfax & Sammons were brought in to reconfigure and renovate the interior.

The result has a timeless modern glamour achieved through a close collaboration between the architects, their client, and the decorator Alex Papachristidis. The owner has a particular interest in the different effects that can be achieved by com-

bining the traditional and new—the incorporation of old style furniture and finishes into a modern shell, for example, or, as in this case, putting twentieth-century furniture, art work, and fabrics into a space expressed in a traditional architectural language. There is a deliberate play here between the feeling of a modern loft space and that of a more conventionally formal interior.

At the wider front of the apartment is an open-plan living/dining room, with superb views out over Central Park through newly made windows. It is entered from a large hall, which has been redesigned to be symmetrical in plan, the front door opening through one of two canted corners (the other has a jib door, behind which a cloak closet is neatly concealed). The architects have introduced new paneling and

Kitchen.

RIGHT *The dining end of the principal room, with breakfast table in bay window. The timber fittings were designed by Fairfax & Sammons.*

moldings, and a floor of American white oak, which Alex Papachristidis had stenciled with a pattern of rings and squares to make a striking impact. One subtle alteration was to narrow the doorway from the hall into the main room by thickening its jambs, so that the opening now aligns with the double window opposite overlooking the park.

The architectural detail of the main interconnecting living/dining room has been deliberately muted so as not to compete with the wonderful park views that fill the windows. Mr. Papachristidis has created, in a clean, understated manner, a slightly Parisian feel, keeping the decoration traditional, with a 1940s edge. This works well with the neutral palette of soft earth-based colors—grays, chocolate browns and oatmeals—and with the pale silk curtains, off-white painted joinery, and mostly twentieth-century furniture bought in Paris and New York. The rugs, laid over exposed oak floorboards and featuring

FACING PAGE *Master bedroom with faux bois French wallpaper and textiles inspired by David Hicks.*

RIGHT *Master bathroom.*

BELOW RIGHT *Detail of guest bathroom.*

two different patterns woven in the same mushroom and taupe colorways, were specially made in Tibet using a combination of wool and silk for textural effect. The dining room's beamed ceiling has been coffered and the former rather inelegant paneling replaced with simpler wainscoting to dado height beneath chocolate brown upholstered walls. Other fittings, such as bookcases and chimneypiece, have been replaced with well-proportioned new ones to designs by Fairfax & Sammons.

The architects have altered the treatment of the pilasters down the long wall facing the park, so that they do not so obviously break up the space, and the room feels more streamlined. At the living room end, the plain white walls remain unpaneled, and the original flamboyant chimneypiece has been replaced with a more restrained marble one, purchased by the owner.

From the opposite side of the hall, a passage leads to the more tightly configured rear half of the apartment, which contains the master suite with marble clad bathroom. There is also an office with a Moroccan day bed in an alcove, allowing it to double as a guest room, and an anteroom to the master bedroom serving as a small office. These rooms are decorated to feel cozy and internalized, because there is no view from the rear of the apartment. The master bedroom, decorated in a palette of chocolate browns, grays, creams and silvers, mixes a *faux bois* French wallpaper with geometric patterned curtains and carpet inspired by David Hicks.

The kitchen, a narrow space running down the south side of the apartment, is lined with Fairfax & Sammons's high quality kitchen millwork—carefully detailed drawers, cupboards, and other storage spaces combined with modern appliances. What is now the kitchen passage linking it to the hall has also been carefully fitted out with new floor-to-ceiling storage cupboards.

The combination of a modern aesthetic with classically detailed finishes is a feature of several of Fairfax & Sammons's urban projects. It can be seen here to particularly smart and stylish effect.

A FRENCH PROVINCIAL-STYLE MAISONETTE

WEST VILLAGE
NEW YORK, NEW YORK, 2006

Detail of new limestone chimneypiece and cabinetry in living room.

FACING PAGE *Living room, with salvaged old French doors opening into garden.*

It is probable that the space that was transformed to create this unusual residence of two small but lofty rooms was used as store to service the old nearby shipping trade during the nineteenth century. It occupies the ground floor of an apartment block one short block from the Hudson River, but it might be part of a *bastide or mas*, so redolent is its character of old French farmhouse interiors.

This project was rather different from Fairfax & Sammons's usual city work, not only for its rustic Mediterranean aesthetic, but also because it was mostly directed by the owner herself. It was Dona Just's guiding vision to contrive a farmhouse atmosphere where others might have created a smart but sterile urban flat. An advertising executive with a love of outdoor pursuits, Dona wanted a city retreat that would feel casual and reflect her European heritage. She engaged Fairfax & Sammons to provide the essential architectural input, and they created a main kitchen/living room that runs through to a charming courtyard garden, with a bedroom opening off one side. At the other end of the main room, above the kitchen area, a gallery provides additional sleeping or storage space, reached by a handmade wooden ladder; the bathroom is fitted into the corner between the bedroom and the kitchen.

The main room and the bedroom have tall, glazed French double doors of about 1900, which open onto the garden; a third matching pair is set into the large opening between the two rooms. They are hung with loose linen curtains and kept open for much of the year, so that the garden (which is the same size as the apartment) and interior merge, and the rooms feel cool and airy. The architects designed a simple but solid limestone chimneypiece to provide the main focus to the living room; in winter, an open fire glows from the grate within its multicolored tiled surround.

The key to this apartment's attractive rustic style is artisan Robert van Nutt's wonderful timberwork—pine doors and shelves, kitchen worktops of walnut and additional quirky touches, such as a French-style post box to disguise the wall-mounted telephone, a wooden box over the front door spyhole, and a framed blackboard to hide the electric panel. These fittings, stained rather than painted to emphasize their natural patina, are all the more impressive since Mr. Van Nutt is actually a professional illustrator, who only relatively recently took up joinery. He researched all the details from traditional French designs, and drew them up in a series of delightful sketches, several of which are reproduced here.

FACING PAGE *Living room looking
toward kitchen and loft.*

ABOVE *View into bedroom.*

FOLLOWING PAGES *Robert van Nutt's sketches
for his timber fittings in the apartment.*

The choice of fittings and finishes was largely the owner's own, underlining her decorative flair and affinity with the rustic French style she has sought to emulate. The apartment is furnished with French antique furniture and has light fittings in a suitable style from Circa Lighting. The coarse ceiling beams are left unpainted and the walls are finished in the traditional European style of rough plaster colored with natural pigments—work which was done by the local artist, Mark Turgeon. French limestone from Paris Ceramics sur-

rounds the sink area, and the floors are laid with antique terracotta tiles, with decorative metal grilles over the heating ducts.

This inspirational project was the result of a happy collaboration between the owner, architects, and an "artist of all trades." Together they have transformed two previously undistinguished narrow rooms into something special and quite unexpected, transposing the timeless atmosphere of the Mediterranean provincial style to the heart of New York.

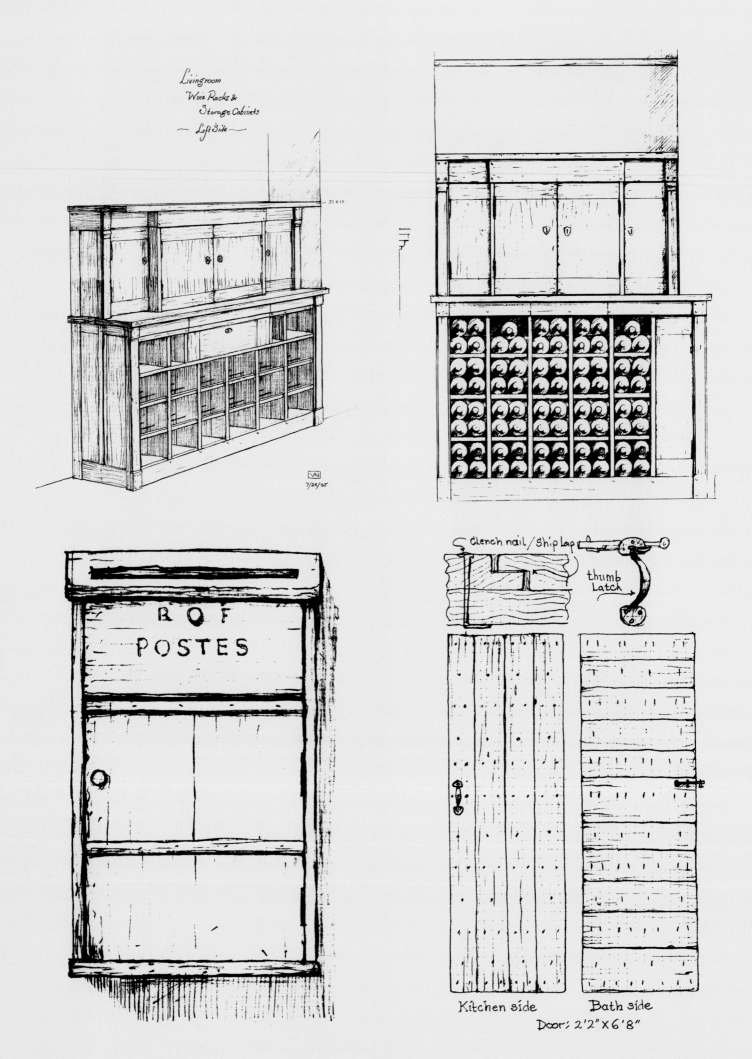

Livingroom
Wine Racks &
Storage Cabinets
— *Left Side* —

51 X 13

7/24/05

R O F
POSTES

Clench nail / Ship lap

thumb
Latch

Kitchen side   Bath side
Door: 2'2" X 6'8"

SOUTH ELEVATION

GARDEN SHED
JUST RESIDENCE

A

B

93

60

H₂O

30

7

A 25

20 B

55½

179

A Long Island Beach House

ISLE OF WIGHT
LAWRENCE, NEW YORK, 2005

PREVIOUS PAGES *Garden façade seen from the marshland to the east.*

LEFT *Library with new painted wooden chimneypiece.*

ABOVE *Kitchen.*

Fairfax & Sammons's renovation of this shingled beach house could be more accurately described as a "creative reconstruction," since the original dwelling house had been so badly altered over the years that it needed a fairly drastic intervention. The result reflects the architects' conversance with the history and architectural character of the Isle of Wight, the enclave in Lawrence within which Albert Place is located. The pocket of marshland overlooking Long Island's South Bay was colonized in the late nineteenth century by a fashionable set of New Yorkers as *the* place to escape to from the city for weekends and holidays. It had formerly been part of the Rock Hall Estate, which was developed in the eighteenth century by the Antiguan sugar trader, Josiah Martin; his handsome mansion still stands, now converted as a museum. Improbably, given the proximity of JFK Airport, and the sprawl of industrial wasteland and middle class suburbs that has encircled the Isle of Wight, the enclave is still fiercely protected by its property holders, many of whom descend from the original families.

This house belonged to a genre of late-nineteenth-century "artistic" cottages designed in the Shingle style by architects such as Bruce Price and Stanford White. As remodeled by Fairfax & Sammons, it recaptures the spirit of its predecessor

LEFT *View of upstairs hall.*

BELOW LEFT *Master bathroom.*

FACING PAGE *Master bedroom with oriel window overlooking the Buttermilk Channel.*

and remains true to the existing footprint. The principal block, with its distinctive stepped gable, retains its original form, but the entrance has been moved from the south side to the street front, and it has a new timber porch. This was designed by Richard Sammons to suggest the Aesthetic Movement origins of the house, with columns in the manner of Eastlake and a sunburst in the pediment. Other references to the style include a cupola ventilation fleche on the roof ridge and a three-light oriel to the upper room in the new east extension. The windows have been appropriately redesigned, with small panes in their upper sashes, single sheets of plate glass below. The whole building is clad with cedar shingles, which will soon weather to a lovely silvery tone. In places they are scalloped, or molded around the cheeks of a small opening, and between the floors an intermittent diaper pattern breaks out.

The original house was characterized by an informal grouping of irregular wings, which gave it the appearance of having developed piecemeal with additions of varying dates. This is a feature that has been carried through to the remodeled version, which has wings occupying the same positions, but rebuilt on a larger scale. The main north/south block has a two-story pedimented rear extension from which a family room opens onto the terrace. The oriel window to the master bedroom above has splendid eastern views over the lawn and a small brook to the reedy marshland that borders the inlets from the Atlantic Ocean.

The sunroom, which formerly projected under a catslide roof, has been replaced with a more substantial structure on the southeast corner. This, too, has French doors opening onto the terrace, and its flat roof has been made into a balustraded balcony for the bedrooms above. To the north, the garage wing has been remodeled as a two-story extension, slightly set back on the main front, and again with a flat roof and balcony. Robustly corniced and crowned with a timber balustrade, it is presided over by an ogee-roofed tower room.

Inside the house, the decorator Katherine McCallum of McMillen Inc. has introduced white-painted joinery and beadboarded or paneled ceilings, combined with floating curtain fabrics and pale paintwork to sustain the impression of a light, airy beach house. This is overlaid by the slightly grander country house look conveyed by the owners' comfortable furnishings and antiques. The skill of Fairfax & Sammons's work on this project has been to aggrandize the house and enhance its appearance without losing sight of the unpretentious mood and Aesthetic Movement influences that characterized the original building.

ELEVATION, PROPOSED

ABOVE *Architect's drawing of front elevation.*

BELOW *North wing with roof terrace.*

FACING PAGE *New entrance porch, designed to suggest the Aesthetic Movement origins of the house.*

A Vernacular Country Retreat

PHANTOM FOX FARM
MIDDLEBURG, VIRGINIA, 2003

PREVIOUS PAGES *The east-facing entrance façade, with a new portico and heightened north wing. To the right are new staff lodgings.*

ABOVE *Perspective rendering of entrance approach by Peter Lorenzoni of Charles Stick Landscape Architect, Inc.*

BELOW LEFT *Site plan.*

FACING PAGE *Living room with new roof structure and chimneybreast, and a view through full-height window/door openings of the Blue Ridge Mountains.*

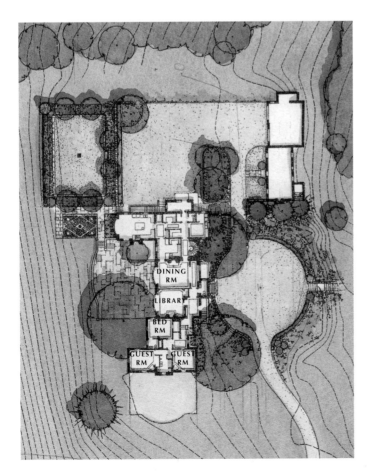

Of all the houses with which Fairfax & Sammons have been involved, none has a more beautiful and unspoiled rural setting than this country retreat overlooking the foothills of the Blue Ridge Mountains. It stands among rolling wooded fields, surrounded by large country estates in the fox hunting country of Middleburg.

The owner, who has various business interests and runs a charitable foundation, is the scion of a prominent old Chicago family. It was his grandfather who first acquired property in Virginia, and the road to the house is named after him, although the house itself, which was built in the 1940s as a modest hunting box, belonged to different owners. Despite being cheaply built of fatly mortared, unrendered concrete blocks, and having few softening features, it possessed, even before the recent remodeling, a quaint charm. Designed by an architect with a reasonably sophisticated understanding of the local vernacular, it was modeled on the Salamander House, a neighboring property dating from the 1920s.

The present owner was a tenant for 10 years before he bought the property in 1999, and in recent years had used it very much as a masculine retreat, a place where he could come to hunt and spend time in the country (his main home is in Georgetown). But in 1999 he commissioned Fairfax & Sammons to enlarge the house and improve its appearance, to upgrade the domestic facilities and open up the wonderful

Kitchen with new west-facing bay window, which replaced a boiler room.

views to the west. He wanted to make it feel more like a permanent home, where his wife, too, would enjoy spending more time.

The house conforms, in its cottagelike vernacular idiom, to the principle of a five-part Palladian plan. The central three-bay block contains the living room on the piano nobile over dining room and library, flanked by lower "pavilion" wings accommodating bedrooms and kitchen quarters. These unmatching wings extend back in L-plan to embrace a terrace on the west front, and there is a staircase in each of the linking bays, the main one on the right being an elegant wheel stair relocated to this position in the recent scheme. The house is a low-slung two stories, and, because it is built on a sloping site, the new Colonial-style portico on the east front, which leads directly into the living room from a charming transverse oval entry, is elevated over a raised basement, whereas on the garden front the lower level stands a full story above ground. The gradient of the ground at the front has now been increased to reduce the flight of steps up to the portico, which allows the new porch to be a more inviting feature and marries the entry level of the house to the grade. This critical move also diminishes the perceived size of the building upon arrival.

Fairfax & Sammons have retained the approximate form of the original house, but have rebuilt the north wing on two stories to accommodate a larger kitchen/service area and master bedroom suite. Heightening this wing also helped emphasize the asymmetrical, picturesque grouping of the ensemble. They have also redesigned elements of the internal plan and replaced all the internal finishes.

With her interest in regional variation, Anne Fairfax has responded sympathetically to the characteristic features of the local vernacular that formed part of the 1940s design. She has preserved or replaced the red tin (or terne) roofs, and ensured that the massive, projecting stone chimney stacks remained a feature of the exterior, also adding two new chimneys—one at the north wing and one at the service cottage—that match the existing ones in material and character. The walls have now been stuccoed, which is typical of vernacular buildings in the Middleburg region, and an ochre limewash introduced. This, along with new shutters painted red to match the roofs, contributes to the warm tones that are one of the building's most attractive features.

Despite the unpretentious spirit of this place, the new timberwork stands out as being beautifully detailed and crafted. The pedimented portico sets the standard: two pairs of slender Tuscan columns, echoed each side of the entrance by engaged

columns slightly more than half in the round, with a door case incorporating slightly convex reeded pilasters. It leads into the small oval vestibule, beyond which the living room runs across the full three-bay width of the central block.

This room has been spectacularly transformed by opening out the ceiling space to contrive a more interesting roof structure: new wooden painted trusses have been inserted and the flushboarded sides overlaid with panels. These have been painted cream, as has all the joinery in the house. Three openings—an elegant sash window with slim glazing bars, flanked by French doors onto balconies—extend right down to the floor to take full advantage of the splendid western views out over rolling country to the distant hills. At the south end a fireplace with a projecting chimney breast has been introduced, which improves the room's proportions by creating recesses on each side, now furnished with antique painted bookcases. The floorboards have been replaced in American white oak, quarter-sawn to random widths to impart a wonderful natural texture. Three balancing openings on the east side of the room lead into a pretty study with fitted desks and shelves, the central oval entrance lobby, and on the righthand side a bar with access through to the south wing stair.

The south range, which is just one story, comprises a small, intimately scaled guest wing, with two bedrooms and bathrooms and a sitting room. By contrast, the master bedroom suite on the upper floor of the opposite wing contains his-and-hers fitted dressing rooms, bathrooms, and walk-in closets on a scale, and to a degree of intricate detail that is perhaps surprising for such a relatively modest house. But then, Fairfax & Sammons are masters at interpreting the requirements of their clients, and their clients generally love highly designed vanity units, closets, and bathrooms. The female bathroom shows how ingeniously the architects can design such spaces to fit in without looking awkward. It comprises three sections, partly underneath the eaves of the link between the wing and the main body of the house, the middle section forming a vanity area lit by a pretty pedimented dormer. This space has been given a tiny, shallow paneled vault, with a segmental arch mirrored by the form of the opening to the bath alcove, and that of the paneled wall beyond. It is carefully considered touches such as these that give the more utilitarian spaces of a house that extra lift.

The master bedroom, with a west-facing French door and balcony, has a coombed ceiling, with a drip-edged cornice with beaded corners that steps back into the recess on the west wall. This cornice echoes that of the Delft-tiled chimneypiece

on the south wall. There are pretty glazed display cabinets specially designed by the architects for the corners of the room, one of which swings out to reveal secret shelves behind. Very much in keeping with the bedroom's feminine character is the curtain and bed fabric. This was made specially by Marino Mills in England to a nineteenth-century pattern chosen by Hugh Henry, of the London interior designers Mlinaric, Henry and Zervudachi Ltd., who had it woven in different colors to suit the room.

Mr. Henry, who supervised all the interior decoration work, felt strongly that the charming "highland home" character of the place should be preserved; he therefore endeavored to ensure that the rooms neither became too sophisticated in appearance, nor were made to feel folksy. They are furnished with some good old family antiques, such as the dining room sideboard, cabinet, and chairs, and the walls are hung, most appropriately, with the owner's wonderful collection of equestrian paintings by a British Edwardian artist.

The dining room and library have twin shallow-bowed openings onto the terrace, which already existed, but their Georgian-style chimneypieces are newly made. The dining room's Roger and Goffigon striped cream and sage curtains were part of Mr. Henry's scheme for this room, but the owners have since painted the walls a claret color. A butler's pantry leads into the extensive kitchen quarters in the north wing, which were fitted out with numerous carefully detailed drawers and cupboards at the request of the owner's wife. The kitchen itself has a big bowed window with a window seat facing west, the wonderful view having been opened up only recently with the demolition of a boiler room.

A "groom's cottage" at the entrance to the drive has also been renovated by Fairfax & Sammons to provide extra accommodation. They have used similar materials and colors in a continuation of the cottagelike, vernacular aesthetic. Just to the northeast of the main house is another detached residence—a staff cottage with integral garage. This new building, too, was designed to group well with the complex, with carefully thought-out details, such as stepping the garage wing down and then up before terminating it under a hipped roof, to render it more domestic in appearance. Equal care is dedicated to every element in a project of this type, down to the detailing of the ancillary structures. Fairfax & Sammons's rustic Classicism combines the "formal arrangement of parts with informal materials" in a manner that is particularly appealing in this project.

A BRITISH COLONIAL-STYLE RESIDENCE

GULFSTREAM, FLORIDA, 1996

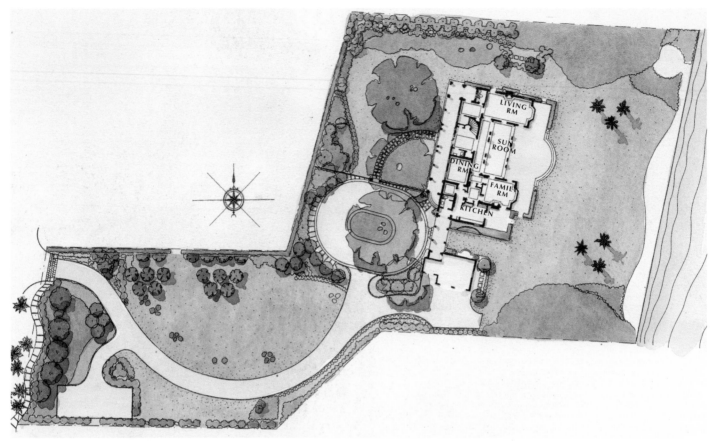

PREVIOUS PAGES *Garden façade with double loggia.*

ABOVE *Site plan.*

FACING PAGE *Transverse hall or gallery.*

FOLLOWING PAGES *Ocean room, formerly an open loggia.*

This fluent exercise in the Anglo Caribbean manner is the result of careful research into the precedents for Colonial Classicism in the tropical South. Anne Fairfax was brought up in Hawaii and ran her own practice in Honolulu for several years, in partnership with Doug Collinson. Her work there included the design of a number of Classical vernacular residences inspired by the local work of Bertram Grosvenor Goodhue, David Adler, and Charles W. Dickey. Fairfax & Sammons's design for this house—her favorite of all their projects—amalgamates influences from Charleston Colonial, French Caribbean/Creole, and tropical British Colonial Revival architecture, with hints, too, of Colonial bungalows in Singapore and Hong Kong. The result is a cool, airy colonnaded mansion with a detached garage pavilion, well suited to its oceanside setting south of Palm Beach.

The house is situated within the residential development of Gulfstream, a prestigious enclave created in the early 1920s by

architects such as Addison Mizner as a place for the rich to come and sun themselves by the ocean and play golf. Mizner's nearby Gulfstream Country Club and other buildings inspired by the architecture of old Spain established the popular Mediterranean/Florida style that the architectural historian Clive Aslet has described as "like a bottled essence of the Mediterranean—infinitely evocative, blended, considerably more potent than the original."

The garden, which is well sheltered by wind-honed plantations of sea grape and banyan trees, is older than the building. The site was previously occupied by a house in the style of Frank Lloyd Wright, but the present owner and her late husband, whose main home is in Charlottesville, Virginia, desired a more spacious holiday residence in the Colonial Revival manner, and commissioned Fairfax & Sammons to replace it. They wanted this new house to protect and make a feature of the magnificent banyan tree that dominates the garden and provides much needed shade to the west front. The landscape was

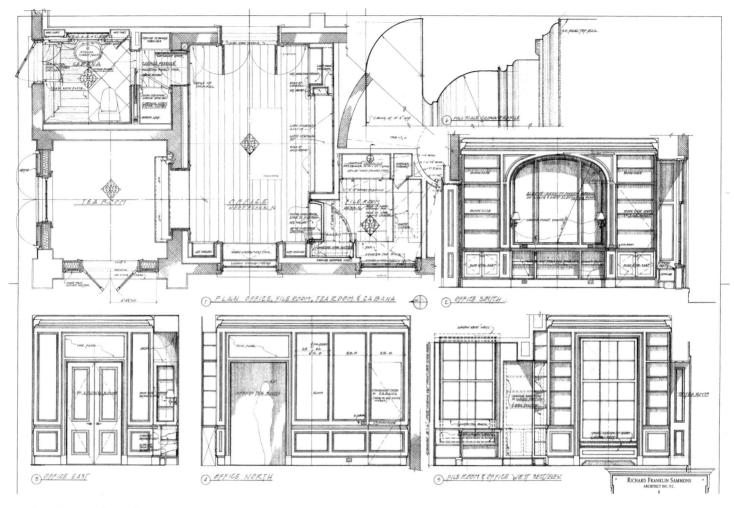

Working drawings for study.

FACING PAGE *The study, painted with* faux bois *sycamore paneling.*

designed by Morgan Wheelock, a prominent Boston landscape architect who successfully integrated the mature surroundings of the former house into the new scheme.

The owner's husband, who died in December 2005, was an executive whose company is involved in energy and finance. A graduate of the University of Virginia, he had a strong affection for the genius of Thomas Jefferson, and this influenced Fairfax & Sammons's treatment of his Gulfstream residence. The incorporation into the design of loggias, occuli, corner porches, Chippendale-style fretwork and octagonal shapes are conscious quotations from Monticello and other buildings by Jefferson.

The entrance façade, with its double verandahs supported on Doric masonry columns, is composed of a subtle balance of solids and voids. Single-story pyramid-roofed pavilions of masonry punctuate each end; the eye is then drawn up to the next level, where a pair of flush-sided sleeping porches over the open ground floor loggia—solid over void—contribute to the pyramidal geometry of the elevation. The upper verandah connecting the sleeping porches is lightened with Chippendale-style railings, which create a wonderful play of light and shadow over the surfaces. The juxtaposition of wood and masonry, the rhythm of recessed wall plane pierced by tall sash windows alternating with solid masonry, is repeated on the east front, although here the owners somewhat altered the effect by glazing in the ground floor loggia, and building out onto the verandah above to create an extra room on each side of the central bay.

The shallow-hipped, broad-eaved roof (designed to divide rain water four ways and to provide shade on all sides); the double, gallery-like verandahs and sleeping porches (floored with a tropical hardwood impervious to rot); the extensive use of louvers and latticework, and the Bermuda chimneys are all key features of the Anglo-Caribbean style. Such houses are designed to provide an escape from the intense heat, while taking advantage of remarkable ocean views, and to withstand the

Guest bedroom overlooking ocean.

FACING PAGE *Guest bedroom in half-octagonal extension at south end of house.*

damage wreaked by regular hurricanes. The Gulfstream residence has a heavy, fireproof concrete roof—of the type originally developed for the restoration of Colonial Williamsburg—which masquerades convincingly as wooden shingles.

The entry sequence was designed to delay the thrill of the first sight of the ocean. Approaching from the south side, you enter the corner pavilion porch and pass along the loggia before reaching the elliptical-arched entrance at the center. Here, glazed double doors with side lights beneath a Federal-style fanlight provide an axial view right through the house, so that one can stand at the entrance and see the ocean pounding on the beach beyond the lawn on its far side.

The entrance leads directly into the stair hall, with the staircase on the northeast corner rising in an elegant curve over a jib-doored closet. A transverse gallery links the two ranges that project eastward on each side of the oceanfront—the drawing room in the north range, balanced on the other side by the family sitting room. Both have tall, canted bay windows com-

manding the spectacular sea view. Between these two wings on the east front is the ocean room—an airy sitting room that was formerly a loggia, with a timber boarded ceiling and elliptical-arched openings, now glazed in. The elliptical arch is a unifying element throughout the house. It defines the recess in the office, a small room that opens off the west end of the drawing room and is painted with *faux bois* sycamore paneling.

It also defines the gallery arcade, and the arches opening through to the formal and informal living areas at either end of the gallery. These arches make inventive use of Classical detail. An informed eye will notice the way an architrave turns to become an impost to an arch, and the unusual but attractive way a keystone engages with its cornice. Throughout the interior, the cornices have coved soffits—a Greek detail that affects the way light plays on the different elements to impart a sense of extra height.

The dining room and family sitting room/library open off each side of the gallery to the south of the stair hall. The latter,

Looking down the loggia toward the entrance gate on the west elevation.

RIGHT *View of house from motor court.*

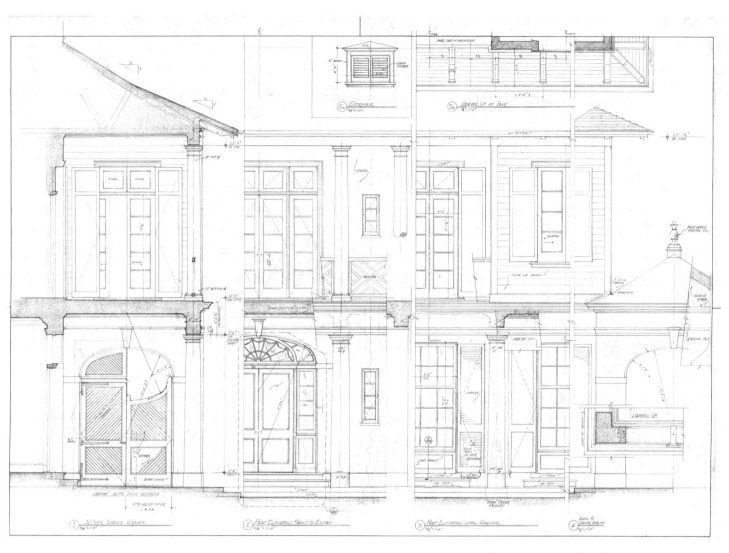

Working drawing of garden/entrance elevation.

FACING PAGE *View from the entrance right through the house to the Atlantic Ocean on the east.*

on the seafront, is a particularly handsome room, paneled with cypress wood that has been pickled to a pale pinkish color to enhance its beautiful grain. The chimneypiece, of the same timber, is decorated with a frieze of interlocking circles, a reference to Batty Langley, and there are bookshelves and a "pots in slots" alcove over the door incorporated into the paneling. In dramatic contrast to this calm room is the red lacquered bar that opens off it to the west; this leads into the kitchen at the south end of the house.

Leta Austin Foster decorated the interior using white voiles and pretty floral fabrics. The master bedroom, which has windows on three sides and a balcony onto the ocean, has a tray ceiling—a practical feature in Colonial architecture—which allows the heat to rise up into the coomb. A series of dressing rooms opens off this room, with the bathroom leading through to one of the bead-boarded sleeping porches. At the other end

of the house is a particularly charming guest bedroom in the shape of a half octagon, with dado paneling and a tented, bead-boarded ceiling. Louvered shutters to the windows, which include a pair of occuli, and to the French doors onto the balcony, open back in the conventional manner, although in many of the other rooms they slide into the walls like pocket doors.

Also provided by Fairfax & Sammons is an inventive piece of furniture that stands on the landing at the top of the stairs—a faux wood painted cabinet, somewhat Soanian in its use of mirrors and in the detail of its pediment, that contains tea-making facilities and a bar. Designed by William Oster, another talented architect in their team, it demonstrates the impressive range of Fairfax & Sammons's output.

Here on the oceanfront at Gulfstream, this handsome stuccoed residence is one of the architects' most successful exercises in the Colonial Revival style.

A Palm Beach Estate

SOUTH OCEAN BOULEVARD
PALM BEACH, FLORIDA, 2000

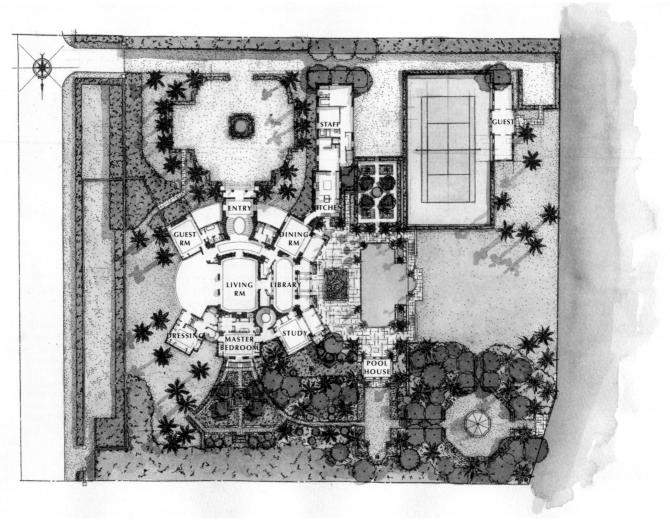

PREVIOUS PAGES South-facing entrance portico positioned midway between the two levels of the house.

ABOVE Site plan.

BELOW Working drawing for drawing room chimneypiece.

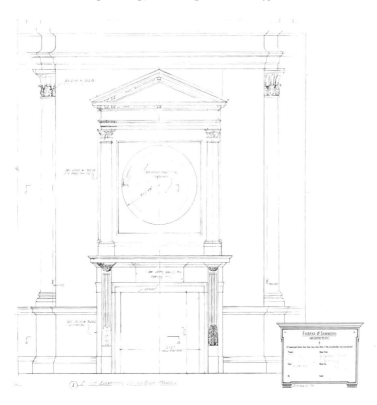

FACING PAGE Drawing room with Corinthian capitals and overmantle carved by master carver, Dick Reid. The painting of Marilyn Monroe is by the Canadian artist, Tony Scherman.

The opening in 2005 of a Fairfax & Sammons office in Palm Beach reflected the firm's growing presence in the South. Among the prestigious Florida residences with which the architects have been involved, one of the smartest is this colonnaded beach palace for a media baron and his journalist wife. Remodeled from an existing house, this glittering white mansion is an impressive addition to the parade of architectural confections that lines Florida's most prestigious thoroughfare. It occupies a slight incline between the ocean and Lake Worth, and has a private tunnel running under South Ocean Boulevard to its own Atlantic beach.

The house started life as the Hans Fischer Residence, built in 1970 to a design by John L Volk, one of a group of architects prominent in Palm Beach in the 1960s and 70s. The plan comprised a long, elliptical-ended central living space, with hip-roofed wings projecting at splayed angles from the corners. Unbalancing the symmetry, a long, two-story service and garage wing was added to the southwest.

Fairfax & Sammons kept the bones of Volk's butterfly plan, but remodeled the entire building. They classicized the exterior and refitted the house with exquisitely detailed interiors,

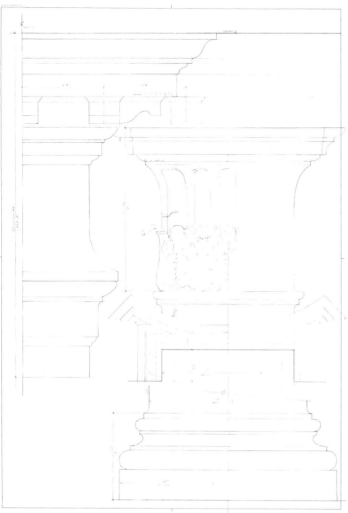

Working drawing for details of the drawing room.

RIGHT *Drawing room looking toward entrance hall, with Rococo mirrors and a specially made chandelier from Venice. The giant order is based on that of Diocletian's Palace.*

creating a suitably uplifting place for the owners to escape their cosmopolitan lives and entertain their friends in style.

On the entrance front, which faces south and is positioned midway between the two levels of the house, the architects redesigned the portico, front door, windows, and flanking wings with well-proportioned Classical detail. They replaced the concrete paving slabs of the large motorcourt with pale gravel, and introduced at its center a fountain pool. Other features that have enlivened the exterior of the house include the new windows—Georgian-style sashes with proper architraves and glazing bars replacing plate glass ones—and the introduction of shutters and quoins. The service wing's unattractive mansard roof was also replaced.

Study with view of Lake Worth beyond a pair of Chippendale-style chairs.

Upper loggia/library.

One of the most thrilling aspects of this house is its grand axial perspective, which extends from the inland waterway on the west to the Atlantic on the east. This contributes to the sense of transparency suggested by the architecture. The west side, overlooking the pool terrace, was refronted to create an elegant double loggia with pedimented splayed ends, providing much-needed shade for the rooms on this side of the house, and taking advantage of the splendid eastern views out over undeveloped land to the bird sanctuary across the lake. The powerful sunlight creates strong patterns on the clean surfaces, casting the geometric shadow of the railings onto the upper loggia's coquina stone floor. This Chippendale design works well with the latticed screens and trellises that ornament the terrace and its buildings, and the fretted design of garden furniture and gates. Seen against the colonnade, these pierced and patterned surfaces contribute to the lightness and rhythm of solids and voids that is one of the most delightful features of the building.

For the landscape designer, Charles Stick of Charlottesville, Virginia, the transparency of the east/west axis took precedence over the garden design. He conceived the landscape on

the west side as a simple and straightforward progression from pool to lake, with a stretch of lawn lined with coconut palms between. A parterre of clipped yaupon holly was made on the terrace, designed to be seen from the rooms above. The pedimented pool pavilion, with latticed arched screens, was designed by Fairfax & Sammons, as was the two-story guest house to the southwest. On the east side of the house, a statue of Neptune carved by the Albanian sculptor Andrian Melka was positioned dramatically to be seen against the backdrop of the ocean.

Inside, the architects worked with the interior designers David Mlinaric and Hugh Henry of the London based firm Mlinaric, Henry and Zervudachi Ltd., which has decorated most of the owners' houses. They, like the architects, understood the lifestyle of these unusual clients—their strong interest in books and enjoyment of entertaining—and they responded well to accommodate these needs. The two firms collaborated on another project for the same owners—their apartment in New York (see page 128). Both properties have now been sold, but they are described here as they were before they changed hands.

At their Florida estate, the owners wanted to convey a slightly Colonial feel, and the interior was given a complete makeover to suit this theme. Despite the size and grandeur of the rooms, the decor was kept relatively simple, with breezy silk or unlined linen curtains and pale painted paneling creating a fresh, airy ambience. A more luxurious style was adopted for the bedrooms.

The entrance hall leads to an oval stairwell, from which stairs embellished with French bronze railings from Atelier St. Jacques lead up and down. Ascending half a level to the piano nobile, one reaches a curved gallery or stair landing furnished with torcheres by Robert Adam bought in England. Ahead lies the vast drawing room, which runs on the north/south axis down the center of the house. This is articulated with a Corinthian order, an abbreviated version of that recorded at Diocletian's Palace by Robert Adam. The capitals were carved by Britain's leading master carver, Dick Reid of York, who also carved the imposing overmantle to a design modeled on one at Harewood House in Yorkshire. The chimneypiece was designed by Richard Sammons and the overmantle depicts a map of the Caribbean Islands. Among the suitably large-scale

Circular internal stair with view of upper loggia/library beyond.

FACING PAGE Main gallery, with view through to drawing room. The torcheres by Robert Adam were bought in England.

Master bathroom with Soanian vault and lantern.   FACING PAGE *Guest bedroom.*

pieces that dominate this room are a pair of Rococo mirrors (an original, bought at Christie's, and a copy of it), and a chandelier, specially made in Venice.

North of the drawing room lies the master bedroom, decorated with a theme of poppies. This overlooks a series of clipped parterres planted with white flowers in a private sunken garden, and connects with dressing rooms and a study in the flanking wings. Between the private master bedroom quarters and the bow-ended upper loggia room, which was fitted out as a library, a rotunda encases a circular stair leading down to the guest bedrooms below. Opening onto the pool terrace between two rooms is a trellis room designed to suggest a winter garden. The lush oasis that surrounds the house was designed to be experienced as a series of garden "rooms" linked by a path, creating a fitting and harmonious setting for the gracious Classical grandeur of this ocean residence.

TOP *View from pool house to Lake Worth.*

ABOVE *Garden fountain.*

RIGHT *View of pool house pavilion from dining room loggia.*

FOLLOWING PAGES *Aerial view looking east.*

An Anglo-Caribbean-Style Villa

LOXLEIGH
JUPITER, FLORIDA, 2005

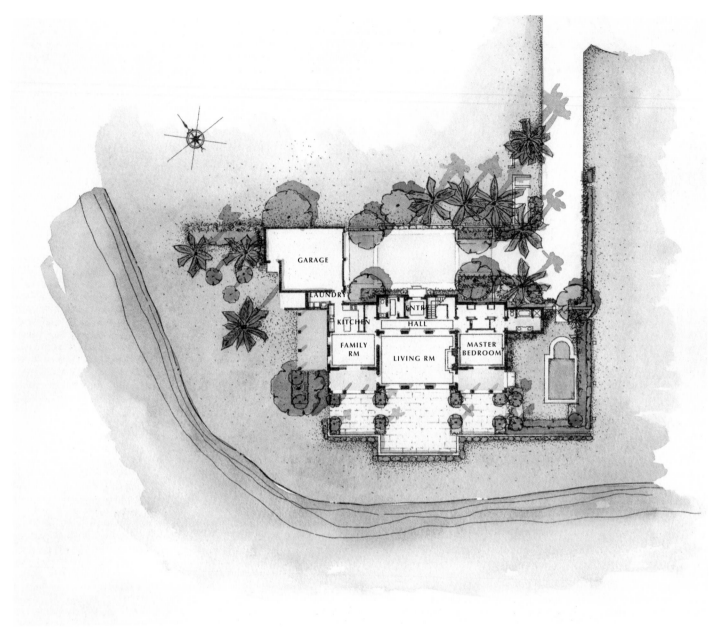

PREVIOUS PAGES *Garden elevation.*

FACING PAGE *Vestibule.*

ABOVE *Site plan.*

This crisply whitewashed villa in the British Colonial style sets new standards for architectural design and planning on residential golfing estates. It is situated at the Loxahatchee Club in Jupiter, one of the more exclusive of the private golf clubs that were developed with unprecedented speed in the 1980s and '90s on the flat, sandy coastal stretch that runs north of Palm Beach in Florida. The 340-acre estate is characterized by some 240 tightly developed lots ranged around pleasantly landscaped fairways interspersed with 12 lakes covering over 70 acres. In this polite, suburban setting, Loxleigh stands out distinctively from its neighbors. It is a house of less than 4,000 square feet, occupying a site of less than a quarter of an acre, yet, viewed among royal palms and

pine trees from across the lake, it might be a large Colonial residence set in its own grounds, perhaps in Bermuda or the Caribbean.

Loxleigh was built as a vacation residence for Jim Utaski, a retired investment manager for a private family, and his wife, Nancy. The Utaskis live in Princeton, but, since becoming members of the club in 1987, they have been coming to Loxahatchee for several months a year to escape the New Jersey winters. In 2001 they were able to buy this plot of land, and immediately set about planning a replacement for the existing dwelling. They had come across Fairfax & Sammons through their interest in Lillifields in Connecticut, which they had greatly admired and considered buying when it came on

The principal living space at the heart of the house, combining dining room and sitting room.

the market. It is no coincidence that the house they chose to build in Florida instead is strongly reminiscent of Fairfax & Sammons's earlier Palladian villa; like Lillifields, too, it draws on influences from the work of Thomas Jefferson, particularly Monticello.

The first ingenious feature of the plan for Loxleigh relates to its positioning within the boundaries of the site. Most of the surrounding residences are characterized by dominant garage protrusions, but here, instead of building a "snout house" flush with its neighbor to the north, the architects chose to set the building closer to the lake on the south side, and to sacrifice a front lawn for a generous drive-in forecourt, at the far end of which stands the garage block. This arrangement makes it necessary to pass across the front entrance on arrival, encouraging proper use of the Federal-style front door. It also means that the house, together with the attached wall and gateway to its east, acts as an effective screen to what lies beyond, so that the signature view across a stretch of water to the sixteenth fairway is delayed until entry.

Loxleigh was completed on a remarkably modest budget, and a notable feature of the project was the excellent working relationship that existed between the architect, clients, and contractor. This led to a strong bond of mutual friendship and respect—a symbiosis that can ultimately be sensed in the finished result. Having clearly set out their brief, the Utaskis made a point of refraining from any subsequent intervention. They have since expressed their appreciation of the high quality of architectural detail and workmanship achieved by Fairfax & Sammons. For the contractor, Dennis McDonald, who has constructed many buildings in the locality, Loxleigh was the first properly proportioned and detailed Classical house he had been involved with, and he learned much as a result.

Even as it was under construction, Florida was battered by no less than three hurricanes. However, despite causing damage to the landscaping, these storms tested an important consideration of the brief: the structure's ability to withstand 120-mile-per-hour winds. Loxleigh has Bermuda roofs of thick concrete tiles covered in stucco, with boarded eaves to diminish the presence of wind pockets; doors open outwards and

View of kitchen from family room.

FACING PAGE *View through loggia to ground floor master bedroom.*

windows are fitted with impact resistant glass in aluminum-clad frames. The house has also been designed to resist rot and termites, with masonry columns and internal joinery using only the most robust timbers—mahogany and Brazilian cherry. Practical features of the Anglo-Caribbean style include projecting eaves and verandahs, which provide shade from the intense heat, and white painted stucco, which serves to deflect the direct sunlight, as well as to emphasize the strong clean lines of the architecture by producing sharp contrasts of shadow and light. Above the well-proportioned sash windows of the piano nobile, the bedroom floor is lit with casement windows for better ventilation.

The plan, which mixes elements of Fairfax & Sammons's Lillifields and Litchfield (see pages 24 and 88), derives from

the transverse hall plan championed by Thomas Jefferson and included among the designs published in *Rural Architecture* (1750) by the eighteenth-century British architect, Robert Morris. Dispensing with the more usual arrangement of an axial corridor running from entrance to garden front, Loxleigh adopts Richard Sammons's favored arrangement of the transverse hall, off which open the principal rooms, with the main living space in a central pedimented block on the garden front. Three large openings leading directly into the living room articulate the transverse hall on its south side. It terminates at each end with a cross wing, recessed on the front and garden elevations. The east wing contains the master bedroom suite, the west the kitchen and family/sitting room, with built-in cabinetry for the kitchen units and entertainment center. At the corners are columned loggias in the manner of Monticello, their roofs serving as porches to the bedroom floor above. These have railings in a Chippendale-style fret pattern, made of durable aluminum tubing but painted white to resemble timber.

The plan of Loxleigh responds to the owners' request that the main living rooms and master bedroom suite should occupy the ground floor on a single level, with a study/office and two bedrooms, bathrooms, and a sitting area for guests on the floor above. One quirky, Jeffersonian touch is the way the stair hall tucks into the bay on the left of the front door, so that the staircase runs up across the window on the front elevation. This arrangement, with a powder room occupying the balancing bay to the right, echoes that at Litchfield.

From the vestibule, which has a shallow vault, the line of vision extends right through the building to the wide green expanse of the sixteenth fairway on the far side of the lake. Because of the house's proximity to the lake, the ground between the two is foreshortened, so that the water appears to come right up to the terrace wall.

The internal arrangement ensures that the ground floor circulation flows naturally into the living room—the principal living space at the heart of the house, with a sitting area around the fireplace at one end and a dining area at the other. The room's lofty proportions—it rises full height to a paneled ceiling in the pitch of the roof—give it a sense of airiness and space. Three pairs of French doors in large, round-arched openings lead out onto the garden terrace, with another pair on each of the flanking walls. With their corresponding occuli in the attic story above, these ensure that the room is flooded with natural daylight, making it feel a wonderfully bright and open space. The whiteness of the external masonry and terrace walling contributes further to this effect by reflecting sunlight back into the room (southern interiors are not as bright as one might imagine, owing to the sharp contrasts of shadow and light).

The interior decorator Lyn Peterson has worked with Mrs. Utaski to sustain a consciously minimalist approach to the decor. She has used creams and whites for the walls and pale upholstery fabrics to achieve a smart but understated look. Pieces of reproduction and antique mahogany furniture are mixed with comfortable contemporary furnishings and lighting. Ornaments are limited—to the large blue and white Chinese-style vases in the living room, for example—and the walls are hung with French pressed botanicals of the 1880s, architectural drawings, antique maps, and sepia-toned photographs, with some large contemporary canvases occupying certain key positions.

The master bedroom in the east wing opens onto the east loggia on the garden front, with its dressing area to the north. A marble-lined bathroom is fitted cleverly into a small side extension, which is screened from view by the wall and gates that enclose the swimming pool. Another clever spatial trick has been to unify with paneled jambs what are in fact three spaces, so that the area containing the dressing room and closets reads as one room.

One of the subtleties of the design is the way spatial connections are made between different parts of the house. This contributes to the order and beauty of the architecture, as well as enhancing the sense of space, thereby helping to promote the feeling of well being that is inherent in a well-designed Classical building. For example, an important visual link is created between the two principal central spaces by making three openings in the south wall of the landing passage, so that it is possible to look down directly onto the living hall from the floor above.

Equal care and attention has been dedicated to the environs of the house, and to the design of the garage block, with its pineapple-finialed pyramidal Bermuda roof, and outriggers that mirror those of the kitchen terrace pergola. On the lakefront, Lutyens-style benches embellish a narrow terrace planted with Box and Dwarf Ixora hedge parterres and palms, and paved with cast limestone slabs. In the loggias and on the entrance front, where the heat is less intense, herringbone brick paving provides an attractive contrast.

One of the delights of Loxleigh is the sense of peace and tranquility that the architecture induces. Sitting on the porch on the south side of the house, looking out over the lake to birds circling above the distant pines, it is almost impossible to believe that Palm Beach County has, in recent years, become one of the fastest-growing regions in the United States.

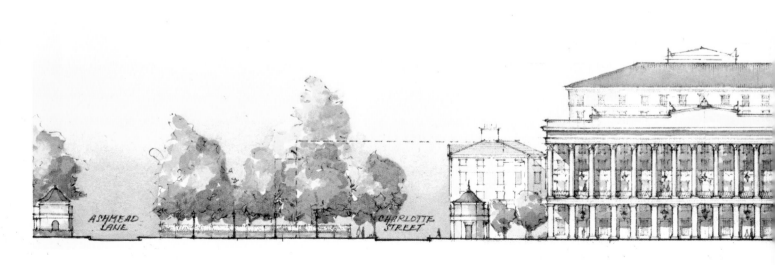

MARION SQUARE URBAN DESIGN PROJECT

CHARLESTON, SOUTH CAROLINA, 2003

243

LEFT AND BELOW *Design for a hotel on Marion Square in Charleston, proposed to replace the building seen in the photograph on the right.*

BOTTOM *Proposed new buildings for Meeting Street, Charleston*

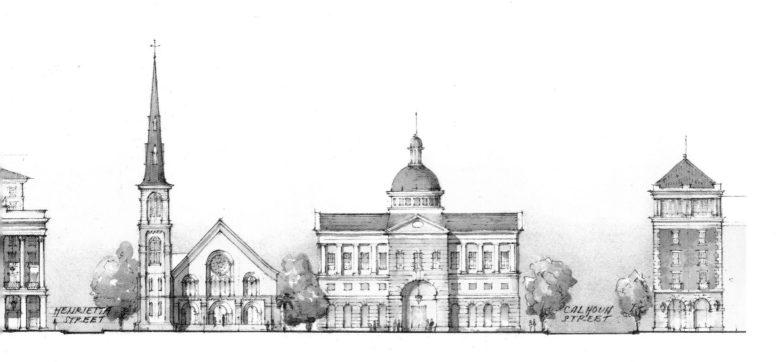

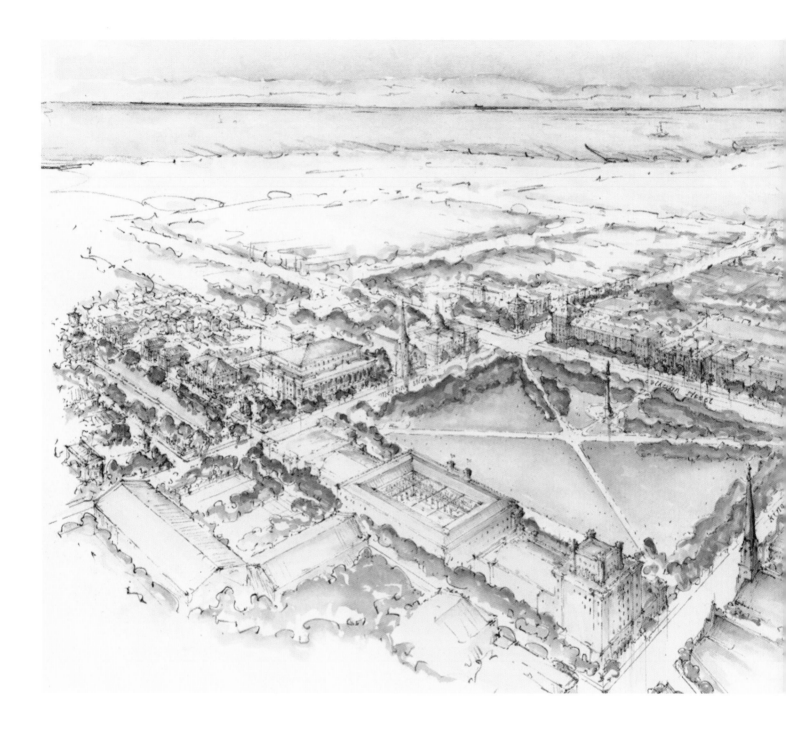

In 2003, Fairfax & Sammons were asked to work with several locally based community groups to create a new vision for the urban fabric around Marion Square in the city of Charleston, and to propose how it might be enhanced and revived. They selected prominent local architects Randolph Martz, Ralph Muldrow, Garey Goff, Hank D'Antonio, and Will Evans to collaborate with them, and took the lead in the final concept. Although only a design exercise, and therefore not constrained by budget and planning restrictions, their proposals for an ambitious remodeling of this key urban space, with a series of imposing Classical buildings designed in the architectural tradition of the city, revealed a sophisticated understanding of complex urban planning and townscape issues.

Marion Square is one of the most important urban spaces in Charleston, and the gateway to the city's historic district. But its fabric has been eroded over the years, and there are gaps in the continuity of the surrounding architecture. One of the few buildings of significance overlooking the square is the Embassy

Suites Hotel at the center of its north side, a building designed by Frederick Wesner in 1842 as the South Carolina State Arsenal, which was converted the following year into a military academy, known as the Citadel, and later became government offices.

Fairfax & Sammons recognized that Marion Square lacked a proper sense of arrival, and that this could be addressed by enclosing the 10-acre space with buildings that possessed a suitable sense of scale and grandeur and created strong architectural vistas. They therefore proposed expanding the Citadel/hotel building with a new wing that would continue along the square where currently a library building proposed for demolition stands. It would terminate the vista from Vanderhorst Street with a tower that would anchor this corner of the square with King Street, and tie in with the adjacent church spire. The lone dominating presence of the existing Francis Marion Hotel on King Street would be mitigated by extending it to the north with a lower extension, and refacing the adjacent

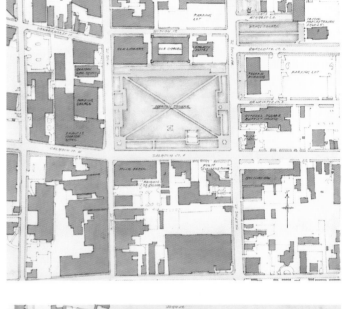

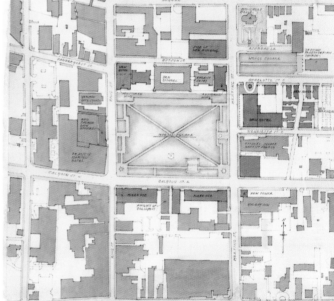

LEFT *Aerial perspective of Marion Square showing proposed new buildings.*

RIGHT *Proposed new building footprints for Marion Square.*

ABOVE RIGHT *Existing building footprints of Marion Square.*

carpark/garage with an office building still lower in height to restore the scale and line of this section of the street.

They proposed replacing the unpopular 1970s Federal Building on Meeting Street, which runs down the east side of the square, with a grandly colonnaded hotel modeled on the historic Charleston Hotel. For the site on the other side of the existing Baptist church, where currently a gas station stands, Ralph Muldrow designed a new bank or office building in a Classical style. On Calhoun Street, a blank wall and uninspiring medley of buildings would be replaced by imposing four- and five-story colonnaded and arcaded buildings for retail use, offices, restaurants, and apartments, and there would be a new Gothic-style police station, and landmark towers at each corner of this side of the square.

By tightening up the urban fabric of the streets along and behind the square, and filling in vital gaps with prominent buildings, the architects showed how Marion Square could regain a sense of coherency and definition, and how the tradi-

tional urban grain of the surrounding streets could be restored. New detached houses on Charlotte Street, designed by Randolph Martz in the manner of many of Charleston's Federal-style dwellings, would blend in with the architectural character of the surrounding Garden District neighborhood. Other considerations taken into account were the mix of building uses, traffic and parking management, the design of sidewalks, tree planting, and the removal of overhead wiring and clutter.

The idea of a masterplan design for Marion Square was intended to spark constructive public debate as to how this important focus of the city center might be revitalized and enhanced. Sponsored by active civic leadership, the Committee to Save the City and the Mazyck Wraggborough Garden District, endorsed by the mayor and widely commended by the public, Fairfax & Sammons's proposals provided a positive model for the future development of this historic area of Charleston.

LEFT *Perspective view of proposed new hotel extension to the Embassy Suites Hotel (the former Citadel) on Marion Square.*

BELOW *Proposed new buildings for Marion Square, including the renovated former Citadel, currently the Embassy Suites Hotel.*

MEETING STREET

THE CRESCENT

POUNDBURY
DORSET, ENGLAND, 2002

Site plan of The Crescent, Poundbury.

Poundbury, in Dorset, England is a remarkable phenomenon. A high-density development in open farmland on the edge of the market town of Dorchester, it proves that it is possible to break the mold of characterless suburban developments and produce a place for modern living that revives the best qualities of traditional urban townscapes. Predictably, given that anything done with the involvement of the Prince of Wales inevitably attracts criticism from some quarters, it has been subjected to negative comment from certain sniping elements of the media. But few who visit Poundbury can deny that what has been completed so far has been a success, and that it offers significant implications for the future.

In the late 1980s, the West Dorset District Council identified an area of about 400 acres to the west of Dorchester for future expansion. This land happened to be part of the Duchy of Cornwall estate, which was established in 1337 to provide an income for the heir to the throne. The Prince of Wales, who has a long standing interest in architecture and design, was anxious that any new development should meet local housing needs without creating yet another car-dominated, zoned housing estate. "I was determined to...ensure that such growth should recapture the organic form and sense of place of our historic towns and villages," he has written. "Poundbury represented a challenge to achieve this without compromising its unspoilt rural setting."

ABOVE *Architect's elevation drawings of The Crescent.*　　　BELOW *View of townhouses in The Crescent*

Elevation drawing for a typical townhouse, designed in a manner derivative of John Nash's Regency urban vernacular.

The Duchy engaged Leon Krier, the visionary architect/ urban planner from Luxembourg, to devise a masterplan, and this is now being carried out in cooperation with architects, developers, and the local planning authority. The guiding principles were to create a rich and varied townscape on a human scale that mixes private and social housing with economic activity. The Duchy imposed a regulating building code to ensure the application of consistently high standards of design and construction in keeping with local styles and building traditions, and the use of sustainable, and where possible, locally sourced materials.

Poundbury was conceived as four urban quarters, each approximating to a different phase, to be developed in response to market demand. Phase 1, begun in 1993, has been complete now for about five years and has already acquired the feeling of a well-settled urban village. Intimately scaled streets of buildings constructed in a mix of styles and materials typical of the area have begun to mellow, and an active community is well established.

Phase 2, which is nearing completion, is more ambitious in scale and in the integration of different uses. It incorporates several factories (cereals and optics), and housing that represents a wider variety of type, size, and style. The design of this quarter is more formal, with wider streets and more civic spaces, the scale of the architecture increasing as it progresses towards what will be the center of the town—Queen Mother Square, designed by Quinlan Terry.

It is in this quarter that Fairfax & Sammons, led by Ben Pentreath, have made a significant contribution. In 2002 they were asked to come up with a design concept for The Crescent, a development of town houses ranging around one side of a curving street that faces north to old Poundbury Farmhouse (now the Duchy's offices) and open farmland. The idea was that the initial concept would be sketched out by the architects, and then worked up to completion by the development companies involved in building this section of Poundbury. But Fairfax & Sammons went a step further and

A townhouse in The Crescent, as completed.

produced approximate plans and full-sized detailed drawings, in order to ensure that the houses would be built to the correct proportions and detail.

The Crescent comprises three-story blocks of two or three houses in a manner derivative of John Nash's Regency urban vernacular, a picturesque Classicism analogous with America's Federal style that defines the early-nineteenth-century character of many residential streets in London and provincial towns across Britain. The substantial scale of the architecture belies the fact that these are affordable houses, with materials and detailing that has been kept deliberately simple. They are built of brown stock brick, stuccoed on the ground floor, with gauged brick arches to six-over-six sash windows on the upper floors. As a contrast, the ground floor windows and Georgian style front doors are set into round-arched openings with molded architraves. The blocks are articulated by stuccoed Greek pilasters, in anta or dividing the long walls, and they have shallow-hipped slate roofs with deep, oversailing bracketed eaves.

The combination of this pleasantly familiar architecture, designed on a human scale, and the sort of carefully thought-out detail that so often falls by the wayside in contemporary developments, such as correctly designed and proportioned chimneys and attractive iron railings, gives The Crescent its sense of place and belonging within the urban grain of Poundbury. Among the rich mix of housing types to be found here, these dignified terraced houses have proved to be among the most popular, and many have already sold.

Having cut its teeth on this relatively small-scale urban development in an English county town, Fairfax & Sammons is now poised to pursue the ideology that inspired Poundbury's masterplan with a similar visionary project for the United States. At a time when there is ever-increasing demand for urban expansion, the lessons learned at Poundbury put the architects in a strong position to develop this important dimension of their architectural practice. Such a project would also present them with the opportunity to add some significant public architecture to their portfolio.

PROJECT LIST

2006

Mr. and Mrs. Charles and Sara Ayers Residence, New York, NY
Renovations to apartment

Belvedere Properties, Southampton, NY
Various Shingle-style residences and outbuildings including lodges, barns, playhouses, and guest cottages on 400-acre Cowneck Preserve (2001 to present)

Mr. Chris Browne Residence, New York, NY
Renovations to apartment in NoHo

Mr. Jim Clark Residence, Miami, FL
New Thai-inspired penthouse at The Setai Condominium

Mr. and Mrs. Alain and Anne Goldrach Residence, New York, NY
Renovations to nineteenth-century wooden townhouse

Mr. and Mrs. Gridish Residence, Ceasaria, Israel
New Classical house on the Mediterranean Sea

Mr. and Mrs. Jeremy and Sara Goldstein Residence, New York, NY
Renovations and addition to nineteenth-century townhouse

Mr. and Mrs. Glenn and Debbie Hutchins Residence,
Manursing Island, NY
New Shingle-style house

Mr. and Mrs. Eric and Paula Madoff Residence, New York, NY
Renovations and addition to Greek Revival townhouse in Greenwich Village

Mr. John Neal Residence, Lexington, KY
Renovation to 1920s Georgian house

Mr. and Mrs. David and Faith Pedowitz Residence, Bedford, NY
Addition to stone house of Scottish Baronial style

Mr. Frank Richardson and The Honorable Kimba Wood Summer Residence, Bedford, NY
Renovations to Colonial Revival house and outbuildings

Mr. and Mrs. Ron and Davita Strachbein Residence, Greenwich, CT
New house in the Georgian style

Mrs. Hunter Smith Residence, Charlottesville, VA
Renovation to 1920s Georgian-style house

2005

Mr. and Mrs. Michael and Diane Brooks Residences, Isle of Wight, NY and Hobe Sound, FL
Renovations to Shingle-style house
Renovations to Bermuda-style house

Mr. and Mrs. Jim and Nancy Clark Residence, Palm Beach, FL
New beach house in the Italian Renaissance Revival style

Chesney Showroom, D and D Building, New York, NY
New showroom for Symm and Co.

Mr. and Mrs. Julian Cohen Summer Residence, Boston, MA
Renovation to apartment in the Ritz Carlton House

Mr. Michael Field Residence, New York, NY
Renovations to apartment in The Prasada

Ms. Dona Just Residence, New York, NY
Renovations to maisonette in Greenwich Village

Ms. Margaret Gardiner Summer Residence, Quogue, NY
Renovations and addition to an eighteenth-century Long Island saltbox

Ms. Victoria Thomas Residence, Reston, VA
Renovation to a new residence

Mr. and Mrs Jim and Nancy Utaski Residence, Jupiter, FL
New Bermuda-British Colonial-style house

Mr. and Mrs. Eric and Trista Wright Residence, Weston, CT
New Colonial Revival house

2004

Ms. Linda Collins Summer Residence, Sneden's Landing, NY
Renovations to circa 1920s stone cottage

Dr. and Mrs. Gaddy Residence, Mount Pleasant, SC
New house in a New Urbanist community, I'on

Mr. and Mrs. Eric Wright Residence, Westport, CT
Renovations to new house

2003

Mr. Jacob Collins and Ms. Ann Brashares Residence and Artist Studio, New York, NY
Renovations to carriage house on Upper East Side of Manhattan

Mr. and Mrs. Julian Cohen Winter Residence, Palm Beach, FL
Renovation to apartments at The Breakers

Ms. Sarah Jessica Parker and Mr. Matthew Broderick Residence, New York, NY
Renovations and additions to an Italianate townhouse

Dr. David Orentreich and Ms. Marina Killery Residence, Cold Spring, NY
Renovations to house

Mr. and Mrs. Frederick and Diana Prince Residence, Middleburg, Virginia
Renovations to a 1930s hunt box and new outbuildings

Mr. and Mrs. Jay and Tracy Snyder Residence, New York, NY
Renovations and new library in maisonette

Ms. Liv Tyler Residence, New York, NY
Complete renovation to an Italianate townhouse

Renovations to 183 and 185 West 4th Street, New York, NY
Renovation to circa 1920s Colonial Revival carriage houses in Greenwich Village

2002

Ms. Adele Chatfield-Taylor and Mr. John Guare Summer Residence, Long Beach, NY
Renovations to beach house, former men's swimming club

Mr. Louis Hager Residence, Cooperstown, NY
New stone 10,000-square-foot Federal house on 600-acre site

Mr. and Mrs. Allen and Claudia Sperry Residence, New York, NY
Renovations to apartment

Dr. and Mrs. Peter and Helen Stovell Residence, Fairfield, CT
Renovation to 1940s Colonial Revival residence

I'on, Mount Pleasant, SC
Two new speculative houses

2001
Ms. Adele Chatfield-Taylor and Mr. John Guare Residence,
New York, NY
Renovation to apartment (Phase II)

Mr. and Mrs. Jim and Nancy Clark Residence, Palm Beach, FL
Renovations and additions to an Italian Renaissance Revival-style house

Mr. Frank Richardson and The Honorable Kimba Wood,
New York, NY
Renovation to apartment

2000
Ms. Stefania de Kenessey music studio, New York, NY
Renovations to composer's studio and office

Residence, Palm Beach, FL
Renovations, additions, and new outbuildings

Residence, South Salem, NY
Renovation and addition to an Arts and Crafts-style house

Mr. and Mrs. Etan Tigay Residence, Greenwich Village, NY
Renovations to a Greek Revival townhouse

1999
Mrs. Nancy Marcantonio Residence, Southport, CT
New Jeffersonian house of approximately 4,500 square feet

Winter Residence, New York, NY
Apartment renovation of approximately 2,500 square feet

1998
Mr. and Mrs. Vito and Rachel Desario Residence, New York, NY
Renovations and addition to 1840s Greek Revival townhouse in Greenwich Village

Mr. and Mrs. Robert and Chantal Miller Residence, Hong Kong
New Palladian villa at the Peak

1997
Mr. and Mrs. William and Carol Browne Residence, Greenwich, CT
Renovation and addition to a Georgian Arts and Crafts house

Mr. Tom Pearsall Residence, Washington, CT
New country house in the style of William Adam

1996
Residence, New York, NY
Apartment renovation of approximately 5,000 square feet

Mr. and Mrs. Carl and Hunter Smith Winter Residence,
Gulf Stream, FL
New 12,000-square-foot Anglo-Caribbean house

1995
Mr. and Mrs. Joe and Barbie Allbritton Corporate Residence,
New York, NY
Twenty-sixth floor of the Carlyle Hotel

Mr. and Mrs. Steve and Cynthia Brill Summer Residence, Bedford, NY
Addition to 1929 Jacobethan Revival house, cottage renovation, new garage, and staff accommodations

Mr. and Mrs. Donald and Patricia Oresman Residence, New York, NY
New private library and residence on Central Park South

Residence, Greenwich, CT
New Shingle-style house, renovations, additions, and outbuildings

1994
Dr. and Mrs. Peter and Helen Stovell Residence, Fairfield, CT
Renovation to 1940s Colonial Revival residence

Mr. Elliot Ruga and Ms. Cathi Hessian Residence, Morristown, NJ
Renovations and addition to existing Colonial Revival house

1993
Ms. Adele Chatfield-Taylor and Mr. John Guare Residence,
New York, NY
Renovation to apartment

Plantation houses and kennels, Easy Hall, Barbados
Renovations and new construction at seventeenth-century plantation

1992
Mr. Robert Pirie Residence, New York, NY
Renovation of 1830s Greek Revival townhouse in Greenwich Village

UNBUILT PROJECTS

2005
Dr. and Mrs. Jack Simmons Residence, Ware's Wharf, VA
New house

2003
Mr. and Mrs Michael and Diane Brooks Summer Residence,
Isle of Wight, NY
New Shingle-style waterfront house

Marion Square, Charleston, South Carolina
Classical design proposal for an urban square

2002
Mr. and Mrs. Eric and Margo Egan Residence, Great Barrington, MA
New house

Dr. David Orentreich orangerie, Cold Spring, NY
New orangerie on the lake

2000
Mr. and Mrs. Jim Clark Residence, Woodside, CA
Design for a new Mediteranean-style house

1993
Mr. and Mrs. Valente Residence, Kiawah, SC
New raised cottage for a retired couple

PHOTO CREDITS

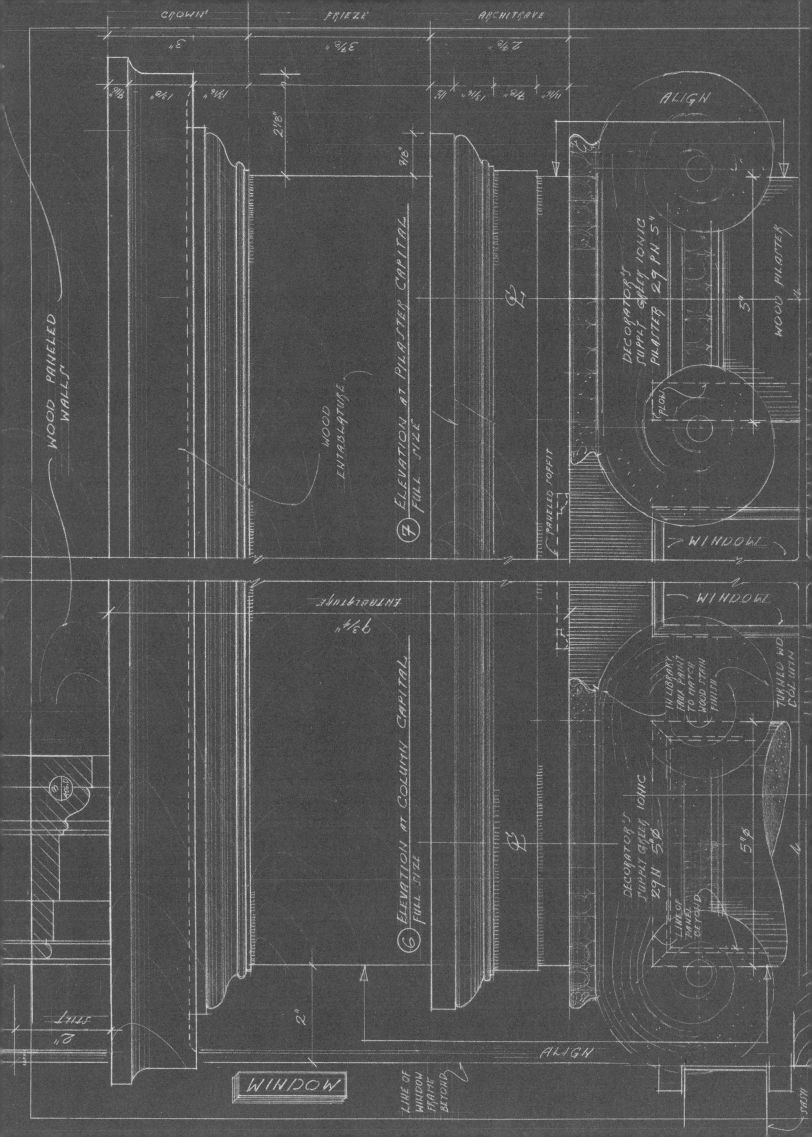